YONI
NETANYAHU

Commando at Entebbe

YONI NETANYAHU

Commando at Entebbe

DEVRA NEWBERGER SPEREGEN

*Illustrated with
Photographs and Maps*

THE JEWISH PUBLICATION SOCIETY

Philadelphia • Jerusalem   5755 / 1995

Library of Congress Cataloging-in-Publication Data

Speregen, Devra.
Yoni Netanyahu : commando at Entebbe / Devra Newberger Speregen ;
illustrated with photographs and maps. — 1st ed.
p.   cm. — (The JPS young biography series)
Includes index.
Summary: A biography of the young man whose dedication to Zahal,
the Israeli military, made him a national hero after he was killed
in the rescue mission at Uganda's Entebbe airport in 1976.
ISBN 0–8276–0523–4
1. Netanyahu, Yonatan, 1946–1976—Juvenile literature.   2. Israel—
Armed Forces—Biography—Juvenile literature.   3. Entebbe Airport
Raid, 1976—Juvenile literature.   [1. Netanyahu, Yonatan,
1946–1976.   2. Israel—Armed Forces—Biography.   3. Soldiers.
4. Jews—Israel—Biography.   5. Entebbe Airport Raid, 1976.]
I. Title.   II. Series.
U55.N46S67   1995
956.9405'092—dc20
[B]   94–48286
CIP
AC

Typeset by Coghill Composition Company

10 9 8 7 6 5 4 3 2 1

ACKNOWLEDGMENTS

My sincere gratitude to the following people, without whom this book would not have been possible: Shirley Newberger, Joel Newberger, Richard Newberger, Jeremy Newberger, Sharon Schoenfeld of Young Judaea, Yaphit Bendori of the Israeli Consulate, Kenneth Kornreich and Marcy Kornreich of Camp Young Judaea, Gadi Epstein of the *Harvard Crimson*, my loving family, Adam and Jordan Speregen, Kate Mason for copyediting and revisions, and Bruce Black of The Jewish Publication Society for giving me the opportunity to bring Yoni's heroic story to American Jewish children.

A very special thanks to Elliot Entis.

This book is dedicated to the memory of Yoni Netanyahu and to all the *chayalim Yisraelim* who have died defending Israel.

Devra Newberger Speregen

CONTENTS

LIST OF MAPS AND ILLUSTRATIONS   *viii*

1   *The Hijacking*   1

2   *Yoni's Roots*   10

3   *Yoni's Early Years*   14

4   *Back to America*   18

5   *The Army*   25

6   *"We've Jumped!"*   30

7   *An Officer*   38

8   *The 1967 Six Day War*   48

9   *A Student*   64

10   *The War of Attrition*   72

11   *The Yom Kippur War*   83

12   *A Battalion Commander*   90

13   *Secret Mission to Entebbe*   96

14   *A Hero Returns*   106

Epilogue   109

IMPORTANT DATES   *111*

GLOSSARY OF HEBREW TERMS   *115*

INDEX   *117*

MAPS AND ILLUSTRATIONS

Page 2   Flight plans of Air France Flight 023 and
              that of the Israeli Army's Secret Rescue
              Squad

Page 5   Operation at Entebbe Airport

Page 26   Israel and its neighbors, including some
              sites Yoni visited and places where he lived

Pages 57–63 Portraits of Yoni

1

The Hijacking

On June 27, 1976, Air France Flight 023—with more than 200 passengers on board—took off from Tel Aviv on a routine flight to Paris. When the plane made its scheduled stop in Athens, several additional passengers boarded the aircraft, including two Arab youths carrying cans labeled "Stuffed Dates" (but probably containing weapons and explosives), a young woman with a ponytail and wearing glasses, and a blond-haired, elegantly dressed young man.

Eight minutes after the plane was again in the air, the two Arabs suddenly stood up and pulled out revolvers. They announced to the passengers in English: "We are revolutionaries and this plane is now our property. We are going to take you where we please." They

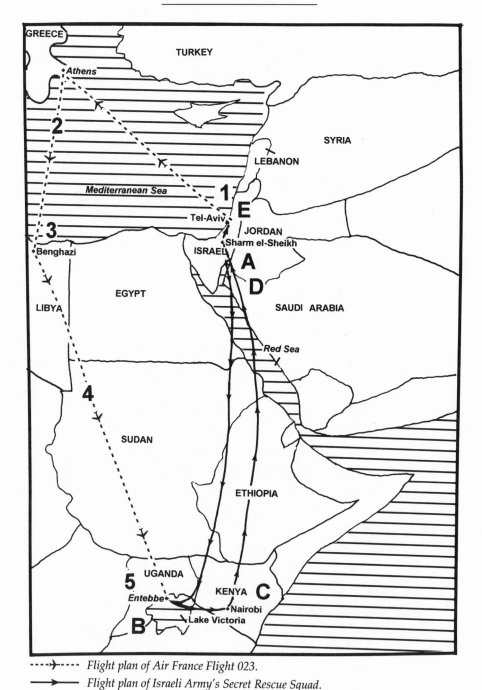

----✈---- Flight plan of Air France Flight 023.
⟶ Flight plan of Israeli Army's Secret Rescue Squad.

ordered the passengers to place their hands on top of their heads and sit quietly.

At the same moment, the woman with the ponytail and the blond-haired man moved to the door leading to the cockpit. The man then kicked in the cockpit door and—as the woman held up a hand grenade with one hand and pointed a revolver at the pilot with the other—ordered the pilot to fly to Libya.

"This is Captain Basil el-Koubeisi of the Che Guevara Force, the Gaza Commando unit of the Palestinian Liberation Forces," the man announced in English over the public address system. "This plane is being hijacked." The passengers sat stunned, in complete silence, with their hands still on top of their heads. Many thought for sure they would be killed.

The passengers were then crowded into the rear tourist cabin. Those who couldn't find seats were forced to sit in the aisles. "I speak to you on behalf of the

------

◄ *Flight Plan of Air France Flight 023.* (1) *Air France Flight 023 leaves Tel Aviv's Ben Gurion Airport for Paris, France, with a planned stopover in Athens, Greece;* (2) *Air France Flight 023 is hijacked eight minutes after takeoff from Athens;* (3) *Flight 023 is ordered to stop at Benghazi Airport in Libya for refueling;* (4) *Flight 023 continues on to Entebbe Airport in Uganda;* (5) *Flight 023 lands at Entebbe Airport's Old Terminal.*

◄ *Flight Plan of Israeli Army's Secret Rescue Squad.* (A) *Israeli Convoy of Hercules transport planes and Boeing 707's take off from Sharm el-Sheikh in the Sinai Desert;* (B) *Israeli Convoy secretly lands at Entebbe Airport and rescues 105 hostages;* (C) *Israeli Convoy refuels in Nairobi, Kenya;* (D) *Israeli Rescue team and hostages stop briefly in the Sinai, before landing at Tel Aviv's Ben Gurion Airport;* (E) *Rescue team and hostages are met in Tel Aviv by welcoming party.*

Popular Front for the Liberation of Palestine," el-Koubeisi told them. "This hijacking is being carried out because of the Zionist crimes in Palestine and throughout the world."

The plane landed at Benghazi Airport in Libya without incident and refueled. Crammed into the rear of the plane, the tired, overheated passengers—many of whom had been on the plane for over twelve hours— waited nervously.

"We will be flying for a few hours longer," el-Koubeisi told the passengers as the plane took off again. "Sit quietly and no harm will be done to you." Six long hours later, the plane finally set down, this time at Entebbe Airport in Uganda, Africa.

Upon landing, many of the passengers sighed with relief—some even applauded! They were sure that their horrendous ordeal was finally ended. But as they were led off the aircraft and herded roughly into an abandoned passenger lounge in a building called the Old Terminal, they realized that it was far from over. While a group of armed Ugandan soldiers surrounded them, el-Koubeisi conferred with several other armed men who were obviously terrorists under his command. As the terrorists busied themselves moving equipment and cartons about, el-Koubeisi told the frightened passengers that dynamite was being placed at all exits, and the entire building would be blown up if anyone tried to escape.

That night, with only a few mattresses available, most of the hostages were forced to sleep on the cold stone floor. The next day, the hours passed slowly. The air was stuffy and clouds of dust rose wherever they

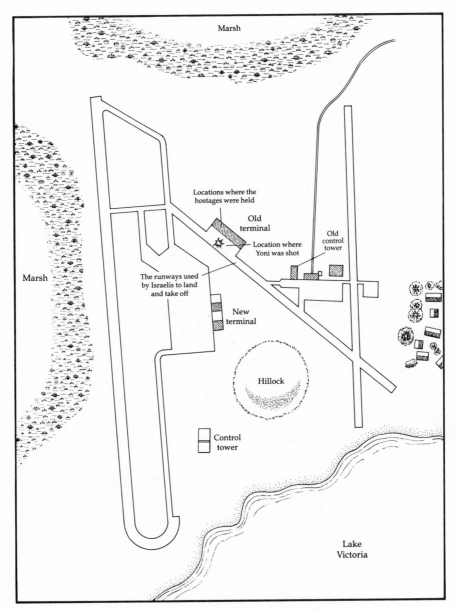

Marsh

Marsh

Locations where the
hostages were held

Old
terminal

Location where
Yoni was shot

Old
control
tower

The runways used
by Israelis to land
and take off

New
terminal

Hillock

Control
tower

Lake
Victoria

Operation at Entebbe Airport

sat. When some of the hostages complained of hunger, some Ugandan soldiers brought them pots of under-cooked meat and potatoes, but other than that, they received very little food.

While the hostages waited patiently but nervously for word of their fate, they were surprised by a visit from a large, highly-decorated man in uniform. Many of the hostages recognized him as Idi Amin, the fearless ruler of Uganda. He proclaimed, "I am Field Marshal Doctor Idi Amin Dada, the man responsible for allow-ing you to be held in Uganda. I do this for humanitarian reasons. I support the Popular Front for the Liberation of Palestine, and I think that Israel and Zionism are wrong."

He went on to reassure the hostages, many of whom were Israelis. "I know that you are innocent, but the guilty one is your government. I promise you that I will do everything to protect your lives."

As time wore on, their overcrowded, dirty, and airless quarters became unbearable and the hostages begged for fresh air and clean clothes. Finally the hijack-ers allowed the children to play outdoors for short periods, limiting their play area to a twelve-foot circle, and the hostages were permitted to wash their clothes in the Terminal bathrooms, but except for these privi-leges, their situation remained unchanged.

Then, on June 30, the third day after the hijacking, the terrorists smashed a hole through a plywood wall, creating a passageway into another, smaller room. As the hostages listened in horror, one of the hijackers read aloud the names of those who were to gather up their things and move into the smaller room—every person on the list was Jewish! Some of the hostages remembered vividly a similar "selection process" carried out by the Nazis in World War II. The Jewish hostages were now even more afraid for their lives.

The next morning, Idi Amin paid the hostages another visit. He told the non-Jewish passengers, except the aircraft crew, to collect their belongings; as an act of good faith, they were being released. "I am asking you not to forget your friends who remain here," Amin said. "You are about to go free, but when you get to wherever you are going, please tell each of your governments to release the prisoners they are holding . . . those on the lists the Palestinians have submitted."

Nine hours later, on July 1, the released hostages landed at Orly Airport in Paris, France.

Those left behind—105 Jewish men, women, and children, including the twelve flight crew members—sat huddled in the Old Terminal building at Entebbe Airport under the watchful eyes of Ugandan soldiers and several hijackers, waiting and wondering, with growing despair, what their fate would be.

Six days after the hijacking—on July 3—Yonatan Netanyahu was seated in the front seat of a black Mercedes 220D. A handsome young man of thirty, "Yoni" was calm and composed, joking with the others in the car, just as if the most important event in his life was not about to take place!

The Mercedes was not an ordinary car, parked somewhere on the ground. Rather, it was a decoy about to be used in a top-secret Israeli rescue mission—"Operation

Thunderbolt"—and it had been stowed in the fuselage of a Hercules C-130 cargo plane next to two Land Rover jeeps. Many hours earlier, that plane, along with three other Hercules aircraft, had lifted off from the Ophir Airfield at Sharm-el-Sheik in the Sinai Desert—its destination Entebbe Airport in Uganda, Africa.

As the plane took off, Yoni—the rescue force commander for Operation Thunderbolt—was excited. This was the type of mission he had dreamed about during his ten years of service in Zahal—short for *Zvah Hagannah L'Yisrael*, Hebrew for the Israeli Defense Army. He knew that Israel had much to prove by successfully completing this rescue raid. This was no ordinary military operation—it was one of the few rescue attempts ever made by Zahal not on Israeli soil. In addition to saving the lives of the hostages being held at the Old Terminal, a successful mission would show the whole world that Israel will never bow down to terrorism.

Yoni was in command of the two units that were to storm the Old Terminal building. He and his men were responsible for securing the building, killing the terrorists and Ugandan guards, and transporting the hostages safely to the waiting rescue planes. The soldiers in the unit called the "blocking force" were being transported on another plane. On board with Yoni were twenty-eight Zahal soldiers hand-picked by him, chosen for their exceptional courage, endurance, and experience. Yoni and these men made up the second unit—the "assault force."

During the long flight over Africa, Yoni walked through the aircraft, shaking hands with each man. One by one, he wished them good luck, reminding them that they were participating in this dangerous mission not only on behalf of Israel but also for all Jews everywhere. Yoni told his men that they should feel proud to have been chosen to take part in this mission, and then—with characteristic caution and attention to details—he made sure that each man knew what he was supposed to do.

As the plane neared its destination, Yoni and several of his soldiers prepared to take their places in the Mercedes, which was to be driven off the plane as soon as it landed. In his final words to his men, Yoni again wished them good luck and said that he had complete confidence both in them and in the success of their mission.

Who was this Yoni? What had happened in his life to make this talented young man so dedicated, so unique, that he was chosen to play such an important role in Operation Thunderbolt?

2

Yoni's Roots

Thirty years before the raid at Entebbe, Yoni was born at Seidenham Hospital in New York City, the first-born child of Benzion and Cela Netanyahu. The account of how he eventually settled in Israel, nearly six thousand miles away, and how he became an ace army commander who fought passionately for the safety and well-being of his country, is indeed an exciting and extraordinary story, one that is intricately interwoven with the history of Yoni's parents and grandparents—Yoni's "roots."

Yoni's paternal grandfather (his father's father), Nathan Mileikowsky, was born in Lithuania in 1880. When he was just a teenager, Nathan heard about *Zionism*—the movement developed by European Jews dedicated to creating a Jewish State. He learned all he could about Zionism, and eventually he became a skilled speaker and traveled all across Russia, preaching in the synagogues about Zionism, driven by the dream of establishing the State of Israel in the biblical home of the Jewish people, the country then known as Palestine.

Nathan traveled to Poland, preaching about Zionism to the Jews in that country. There he met and married his wife Sarah, and it was there that Yoni's father Benzion was born. As a young boy, inspired by his father's speeches about Zionism, Benzion dreamed of the day when he and his family would live in a Jewish State, or at least in the homeland in Palestine that might one day be returned to the Jewish people.

Nathan and Sarah had made plans to move to the Jewish community in Palestine in 1914, but the coming of World War I kept them in Poland. Then, in the Spring of 1920, ten-year-old Benzion and his family began the long, harrowing journey—traveling by train and by boat—across Central Europe to Palestine. With barely enough food to keep them alive, Nathan and Sarah and their two sons finally reached the port of Jaffa in Palestine.

Nathan and his family quickly settled in the *Yishuv*—the organized Jewish section of Palestine, which—like all of Palestine—was under British rule since the end of World War I in 1918. Nathan found work as principal of an elementary school in *Safed*, one of the oldest Jewish communities in Palestine. At the same time he continued to preach about Zionism, traveling across the country and taking Benzion and his brother with him.

Living in Palestine, Nathan became more convinced

than ever that the Jewish people needed its own nation, one in which the official religion of its citizens was the Jewish religion and the official language was Hebrew. In fact, Nathan insisted that only Hebrew be spoken in his home, and he even changed the family's Lithuanian surname—Mileikowsky—to *Netanyahu*, which means "God-given" in Hebrew.

When Benzion was twelve years old, his father enrolled him at a Jewish seminary in Jerusalem. He excelled in his studies, especially history, his favorite subject. In 1929, he was accepted at the Hebrew University in Jerusalem, where he went on to complete a four-year course in history, literature and philosophy.

Over the next ten years, Benzion was busy with his studies and, increasingly, with activities related to Zionism. Articles by him appeared frequently in several Zionist newsletters, and he became a devoted follower of Vladimir Jabotinsky, an important Zionist leader.

During this time, Adolf Hitler was rising to power in Germany, and there was growing evidence that terrible things were happening to Jews not only in Germany but throughout Europe. For this reason, Benzion decided to go to America and join the forces there that were urging all nations to recognize the need for the Jewish people to have their own nation, which would be a place of refuge for the Jews being persecuted in Europe. In April, 1940, Benzion reached Ellis Island in New York.

While taking part in a campaign to raise money for Zionism, Benzion continued his studies of Jewish history, commuting to Dropsie College in Philadelphia, Pennsylvania, from his tiny apartment in New York City. Then one day he ran into Cela Segal, an old friend from Hebrew University in Jerusalem. Cela had been one of the first women enrolled at the university. Following graduation, she had traveled throughout the world. When they met again, Cela was working as a secretary for the Zionist Emergency Council.

Four years later—in 1944—Cela and Benzion were married. It was strange how alike their backgrounds were in many ways. Like Nathan, Cela's father Benjamin was born in Lithuania. He too had emigrated to Palestine—from Minneapolis, Minnesota—in 1911, marrying Cela's mother Malkah there. Cela—the youngest of seven—was born in Palestine, in Petach Tikvah, a town just north of Tel Aviv.

At the beginning of their married life, Benzion and Cela lived in a furnished room on the West Side of Manhattan. They had very little money and spent all their time working. Never once did they put aside their dreams about Zionism; in their spare time, they labored together for the Zionist cause.

On March 13, 1946, their first child was born. They named him Yonatan, after his grandfather Nathan.

3

Yoni's Early Years

Yoni's childhood began in a tiny apartment on Broadway and 94th Street in New York City. Every day, while little Yoni played at his feet, Benzion worked for hours on his Ph.D. thesis. Every night after Cela came home from work, while Yoni slept in his crib, she typed a copy of what Benzion had written that day.

Then, one day in May, 1948, when Yoni was two years old, his parents, along with other Jews around the world, saw their dreams come true—Israel was proclaimed a Jewish State by the United Nations. Six months later, the Netanyahus packed up and sailed for "home" on the American ship *Marine Carp*. During the three-week journey, Yoni and his parents had to share their tiny, cramped cabin with strangers. Cela and Benzion occupied the time playing with Yoni and reading to him. Finally, after what seemed like an eternity, the *Marine Carp* landed in Haifa and the Netanyahus stepped onto Israeli soil. Joyously they made their way south to the home of Yoni's grandparents, Nathan and Sarah, in Tel Aviv.

For the next several months, Benzion searched for work. Then, early in 1949 he was invited to become the editor of the *Hebrew Encyclopedia*, which had offices in Jerusalem. The job paid well and guaranteed the Netanyahu family a comfortable life. They left Tel Aviv and moved to the southern Jerusalem suburb of Talpiot, where they rented a single-story house on "Windy Hill."

When he was older, Yoni spoke of his childhood years in Talpiot as "the best and most beautiful days I ever had." He especially remembered the joy of exploring the huge, grassy fields near his home, looking for ladybugs and playing with the other children.

Shortly after the family had settled into their home on Windy Hill, Yoni learned with delight that he had a new brother—Binyamin, or "Bibi," as the family called him. As soon as Bibi learned to walk, the two boys played together constantly.

When he was six years old, Yoni was enrolled in the Gymnasium elementary school, which was an hour away by bus. Every day Yoni boarded the school bus for the long trip across Jerusalem. It was on these trips that Yoni developed the passion for reading that would stay with him throughout his life.

Just before Yoni's seventh birthday, in 1952, his

brother Iddo was born. A year later Benzion and Cela were able to buy a house of their own. Their new home on Haportzim Street in Katamon—another suburb of Jerusalem—was only a few hundred yards away from Yoni's new school. Yoni was happy there and continued to excel in his studies and quickly made new friends.

The Netanyahus' house had once been part of a wealthy Arab community and had seen its share of battles. There was even a bullet hole in the handle of the front door, which fascinated Yoni and Bibi. They liked to show it off to their friends, making up stories about bloody battles that had taken place right on their doorstep. There was a staircase to the roof, where Yoni often escaped to read a book or just to be by himself. The big tree in the back yard was perfect for climbing.

Yoni and Bibi played endless games of marbles and tag with the other children in the neighborhood, and a war game called "The Greeks and the Maccabees." But the most fun of all was playing *stanga*—a popular Israeli game that was a sort of cross between soccer and kickball—on their large balcony. Yoni played this "street" game often and developed the keen athletic skills that helped him to become an excellent soccer player later in life. Even then, Yoni was a natural leader, whom the other children always wanted to follow.

Though not a religious family, the Netanyahus enjoyed celebrating the Jewish holidays together. Usually they joined with close relatives, neighbors, and friends to observe the *Pesach* (Passover) Seder. Often, on *Shabbat* (the Sabbath) Cela would light the sabbath candles and prepare a delicious festive dinner. At *Purim*, Yoni and his brothers—like most of their schoolmates—always wore costumes. At his kindergarten Purim party, Yoni dressed up as the Persian King Achashveros, Queen Esther's husband, who saved the Jewish people from the wicked Haman.

At the time when Yoni was growing up, most Israeli children were Scouts. The Israeli Scouts, established in 1919, is something like the Boy Scouts and Girl Scouts of America, but boys and girls in the Israeli Scouts are in the same troops, or "clubs," as they are called. Like the American Scouts, the Israeli Scouts participate in all kinds of activities, from hiking and camping trips to volunteer work such as helping at hospitals, restoring wilderness preserves, and taking part in disaster relief efforts. Unlike the American Scouts, in Israel the leaders usually are just a few years older than the members. At the weekly club meetings, boys and girls sing and dance together, do their homework, or just socialize.

When Yoni was ten, he joined the Scouts. He never missed a meeting at the local clubhouse, a beaten-down shack in the Valley of the Cross, that the Scouts had fixed up. Yoni loved dressing up in his official Scout uniform and meeting with the other Scouts in his club every weekend and, often, on weekdays after school.

Years later, when he was grown up, Yoni wrote to his parents that he truly believed his involvement in the Scouts helped him to flourish later in the Israeli army.

4

Back to America

In 1957, Benzion was offered a visiting professorship at Dropsie College in Philadelphia. As Yoni said many sad goodbyes to his friends in school and in the Scouts, the Netanyahus packed their belongings and closed up the house on Haportzim Street. For the second time in young Yoni's life, he traveled across the Atlantic.

On their return to New York City, the family moved into a cramped, one-bedroom apartment on West 86th Street. Yoni had forgotten most of the little English he knew, and he disliked his new American school.

Coming from the peaceful, clean neighborhood of Katamon, the Netanyahu family found New York City noisy and dirty. There was no room in the crowded apartment for Yoni and his brothers to play, and they were miserable and homesick. Yoni missed his friends in the Israeli Scouts terribly.

When the school term ended and summer vacation began, Benzion and Cela sent the boys to summer camp in Maine and began looking for a new home out of the city. They found a nice house close to the ocean in Long Beach on Long Island, New York. There were good schools nearby, and the neighborhood was pretty and clean. Yoni and his brothers were excited and surprised when they saw their new home—they were so close to the ocean that they could smell the salt water.

Autumn and winter came and went quickly. Yoni and his brothers spent much of their free time outdoors, bicycling, skating, fishing, and playing football. In March of 1959, Yoni celebrated his thirteenth birthday and had a Bar Mitzvah at a New York City synagogue. School was fun again for Yoni, but he still missed Israel and his friends there.

Then, a few months later, Benzion's work was completed and he announced that they were moving back to Jerusalem!

Back home in Katamon, because of his outstanding grades Yoni was accepted at the Gymnasia Ivrit, one of the best high schools in Jerusalem. Like his father, Yoni was always serious when it came to studies and dove into his school work with an intense passion for learning that was unusual in a teenager. By their example, Benzion and Cela taught Yoni and his brothers—who were also excellent students—to love learning and to be proud of being Jewish and Israeli.

Yoni was popular among his classmates, and at the age of sixteen he was elected head of the school student body. That same year he was also elected leader of his Israeli Scouts club, *arazim* (Hebrew for "cedars"). Under his leadership, the club's membership grew—from twenty members to well over one hundred!

Just when everything seemed to be going along perfectly for Yoni, Benzion was offered a job as editor of the *Encyclopedia Judaica* in Philadelphia. One autumn night in 1962, Benzion announced that the family would be moving back to America.

Tearfully, Yoni tried to convince his parents to allow him to finish high school in Jerusalem. He reminded them that any Israeli boy or girl over sixteen who was eligible for military service could leave Israel only with special permission from the Ministry of Defense. Benzion was willing to let Yoni remain in Israel, but Cela put her foot down, insisting that Yoni was too young to be on his own. Benzion was able to get permission for Yoni to leave, and the case was closed. With a heavy heart, Yoni had no choice but to pack up his things once again.

In January of 1963, the Netanyahus settled in Elkins Park, a pleasant Philadelphia suburb with wide streets and many trees, and their house was roomy and comfortable. Yoni was enrolled in Cheltenham High School—which had an outstanding reputation. He found the transition to a new school especially difficult this time. Suddenly he went from being the popular, sought-after student body president in his Israeli school to being the "new kid"—and a foreigner at that—slightly confused because of joining classes in the middle of the school term, all alone during class breaks while everyone else seemed to have a bunch of friends to joke and laugh with.

Yoni told himself that it would only be for a while—in a year and a half he would be returning to Israel to enter the army—but at times he felt his homesickness was more than he could bear. Then he would write long letters to his best friend Koshe Karpeles, to an Israeli Scout leader named Rina, or to his former classmates at the Gymnasia.

"My school has about 1500 students. . . . It looks more like the Tel Aviv Sheraton than a school," Yoni wrote to Koshe, poking fun at the "rich Americans" he lived with. "Beautiful even by American standards," he went on, "brand new, and it cost 6.5 million dollars to build!"

"Write me more about everyone in *arazim*," Yoni wrote to Rina. "Write about them in the greatest detail—what are they doing? What are the problems in the troop? Write about each and every group leader."

"There's not a moment here," Yoni wrote in another letter to Koshe, "even the most precious and beautiful one, that I wouldn't trade for my immediate return to Israel. My friends in Israel, my social life there, and above all the land itself—I miss very much."

Over the next few months, life gradually improved for Yoni. He continued to do well in his studies, especially in math and history, his favorite subjects. He made several good friends at Cheltenham, and took part in sports such as soccer and bicycling.

In early spring, Yoni was interviewed by a school-mate for a feature story in the school newspaper, and his social life picked up quite a bit. "Apparently the interview was quite successful," he wrote to Koshe. "I'm being invited to homes, parties, etc., because the 'parents want to meet me.'"

Then, in June of that year, something wonderful happened: Along with two other teenagers from Israel, Yoni was accepted as a delegate to Camp Young Judaea in New Hampshire. Young Judaea—a "sister" group of the Israeli Scouts, composed of American boys and girls of the same age—operates summer camps across the country. Yoni would spend the summer as a counselor, living in a cabin with a group of eleven-year-old American Jewish kids, sharing his experiences as an Israeli Scout through games, songs, and stories.

As the summer days drifted by, Yoni became very close to his young charges. The camp's daily routine brought back happy memories of the good times he'd spent with his Scout troop in Israel. He was happier than he'd ever been since leaving Israel. Most of all, he enjoyed leading a group again.

Yoni's letters to his parents and brothers were filled with details about his daily adventures. He described the hay rides, the evenings spent singing and dancing to familiar Israeli melodies, the canoe trips down Snake River, the thrill of having found a new "best friend" in Elliot Entis, another counselor, and the exciting "color wars," the camp-wide competitive games that bring the season to a close in a frenzy of team spirit.

"I am now riding in a pickup truck which is taking me and my campers to dine at a restaurant as a prize for being selected the 'honor bunk,' " Yoni wrote to Bibi. "I'm not the only one who thinks this is *the* [best] bunk—everyone else thinks so, too!"

Yoni's friend Elliot recalled the effect that Yoni had on the entire camp. "Yoni was there to teach scouting and Israeli culture to the kids. The kids loved him. He was the kind of guy who was full of enthusiasm, excited about everything. And that excitement would rub off on the campers. Yoni was capable of making a fun game out of *any* activity. He always had a 'Let's do it' kind of attitude," Elliot added. "Whatever idea came up, Yoni always said, 'Let's do it!' "

Elliot especially remembered one activity that Yoni enjoyed leading—building towers out of logs and ropes. "The whole idea," Elliot said, "was to teach the kids a bit of Israeli history and culture in a fun way. Yoni would explain that after Israel won its independence in 1948, the Israeli pioneers who built the villages always built a tower somewhere in the village so that they could watch over and protect their homes.

"We used to see which group of kids could put up a tower the fastest," Elliot recalled. "I remember that my group made a fifteen-foot tower with a platform. It was real fun. Yoni was an expert at that kind of stuff."

Elliot also remembers the exciting nature hikes and overnight camp-outs Yoni led. "The kids would all bring their sleeping bags and pillows," Elliot recalled. "Yoni was a master at telling stories around the campfire!"

One particularly emotional time for Yoni that summer, Elliot remembers, was during the Jewish holiday of Tish'a B'av—the remembrance of the destruction of the First and Second Temples, and the Expulsion of the

Jews from Spain in 1492. The holiday—a very solemn day for Jews—was observed by the campers. "Tish'a B'av falls during the summer," Elliot said, "and it was always observed at camp. We had a candle lighting ceremony, and I remembered that Yoni was very different that evening, very quiet and thoughtful. Later that night, he and I had a long discussion about the history of the Jewish people. Yoni was always very concerned with the identity of the Jewish people, and though he wasn't a religious person, he was passionate about Jewish and Israeli history."

In September Yoni said goodbye to all his friends at camp. Many campers promised to visit Yoni someday in Israel.

With one more year of high school left, Yoni concentrated on his studies. He knew that it was important to keep his grade point average high if he were to attend college after his army service. He had already decided he wanted to go to Harvard University in Cambridge, which was not too far from Boston, where his friend Elliot lived.

Away from school, Yoni enjoyed baseball, and he became a rabid Philadelphia Phillies fan. He also liked traveling and seeing the country, and he often visited with friends from summer camp. During the two-week long winter school break, Yoni visited Elliot in Boston.

"We tried to teach Yoni how to ice skate," Elliot recalled, laughing. "And how to play softball, too. Skating and softball were two things Yoni *wasn't* very good at!"

5

The Army

Finally, in June, 1964, Yoni graduated—with honors—from Cheltenham High. At the beginning of July, Yoni said goodbye to his family and American friends and boarded an El Al flight for Israel. Now eighteen years old, Yoni was ready to begin his service in Zahal—the Israeli army.

Every Israeli boy and girl of eighteen—except for the ultra-Orthodox and the physically disabled—must serve in Zahal. This is necessary because of Israel's history and geographical position. Surrounded by unfriendly Arab countries on all sides, Israel has constantly had to be prepared to defend itself.

In Israel, without his parents and on his own, Yoni was both excited and nervous. "When I saw the country [of Israel] for the first time from the plane," he wrote to his parents, "I felt a twinge in my heart. Despite

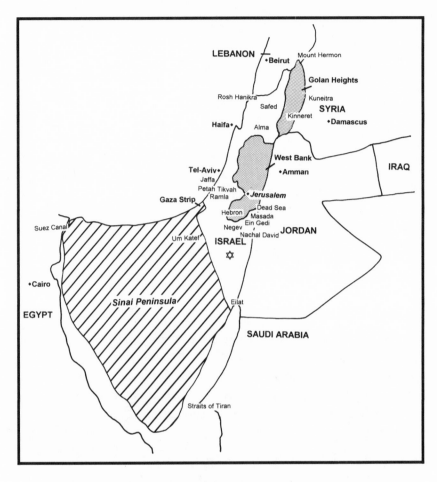

Israel and its neighbors, including some sites Yoni visited and places where he lived.

everything that's wrong here, and God knows there are many faults and evils, it's our country and I love her as I always have."

Yoni spent his last six weeks as a civilian visiting relatives and traveling around the country with friends—backpacking through the Negev Desert, exploring the Old City of Jerusalem, and just lying back and relaxing on Tel Aviv's beaches. Then, on August 10, he reported for duty at the recruitment camp in Tel Aviv.

For the first few days, Yoni stayed at a transit camp, or *Kelet*, with hundreds of other recruits, where he took a series of physical and psychological "aptitude" tests. Although recruits could choose the division that they preferred to serve in, the tests would determine what type of service they were best qualified for—for example, a tank expert, or a mechanical engineer, or an Air Force pilot. While taking these tests—many of which were grueling and demanding—Yoni and the other recruits had to perform daily tasks such as road-sweeping, helping out at mess hall, and guard duty. No one had the time or energy to complain or feel homesick— everyone fell into their cots exhausted at night, and by "lights out" time, most of the young recruits were already "out," sound asleep.

Finally, the tests were over. Those recruits— including Yoni—with exceptionally high scores were shipped off to an Air Force base called Tel Nof for further specialized tests and interviews. The recruits who did well on these tests usually were asked to volunteer for the Air Force, which sought out the most intelligent and able-bodied recruits to train as pilots.

Most of the recruits who qualified were thrilled and eager to go to flight school, but Yoni, who had done well on the specialized tests, had other ideas. "I don't think I'll go into the Air Force," he wrote to his parents. "It means *five years* [in the army]—far too long!" The thought of being a pilot was exciting, but Yoni—who had already decided to enroll at Harvard after his twenty-six months of service in Zahal—knew that this decision was best for him in the long run.

At the end of a long week of tests, Yoni stood at attention with sixty other recruits. When the officer in charge asked, "Does anyone here *not* wish to proceed in flight training?" Yoni nervously stepped forward. To his surprise, he was joined by eight other recruits who evidently felt the same way.

Back at the Kelet, Yoni continued his basic training, performing the typical chores assigned to lowly recruits—like washing military vehicles, cleaning latrines, and scrubbing floors—passing his free time lying on his cot and reading. He had mixed feelings passing up the opportunity to serve as a pilot in the Air Force. He knew it was an honor to be selected, but he also had a gut feeling that there was some other division in Zahal just right for him.

Day after day he watched as his friends and fellow tent-mates went off to different Zahal divisions. One friend joined the Intelligence Corps—he had studied Arabic. Another was snatched up by the Signal Corps, others by the Navy, and still others by the Armored Corps. Yoni wondered, with growing impatience, where *he* would wind up. In a letter to his parents, he confided that he was "going insane" with boredom.

Then, one day during his second week back at the Kelet, Yoni met an officer from the Zahal Paratroops. The officer, after interviewing Yoni, was impressed by his qualifications and urged him to volunteer for this elite division. As the officer described the details involved in becoming a paratrooper, Yoni was intrigued and excited by the regimen, especially by the prospect of learning how to parachute from an airplane.

Paratroops are similar in armies all over the world. Today, instead of parachuting from carrier planes, paratroopers usually are flown by helicopters to combat zones. However, they still must learn this skill, and the training program is one of the toughest, pushing a person's courage and endurance to the limits and beyond. In fact, it is so tough that less than half the recruits who enter the Zahal Paratroop training program finish!

Convinced that this was the right division for him, Yoni decided to try out for the Paratroops. At the end of August, he passed the final series of tests with flying colors. He was now a soldier—if only a rookie—in the Paratroops, one of the elite regiments of Zahal!

6

"We've Jumped!"

Back in Philadelphia, Yoni's parents were proud of their son's decision to join the Paratroops, although they were concerned about the danger involved. While he was going through the grueling basic training course at undisclosed locations around Israel, Yoni wrote reassuring letters to his parents, primarily to comfort his worrying mother.

". . . The paratroop corps is known as a dangerous place to serve, but that's not true. It's [only] as dangerous as any other combat unit. . . . Everything is really perfectly alright," he assured them in another letter. "Don't be frightened and don't worry."

The three-month basic training program was tough and exhausting, but invigorating and physically challenging as well. After two weeks of hard drilling, Yoni was tired but in the best physical shape in his life. Like the other recruits, Yoni fell into his cot exhausted at the end of the day, but he enjoyed the strenuous activity and discovered that he was a lot tougher than he'd thought.

On September 11, Yoni wrote to his parents, "Yesterday marked the end of my first month in Zahal. . . . now I know at last what 'hard life' is, although everyone says that this is nothing compared to what is yet to come!"

Unable to keep up with the strenuous training, many of the recruits were transferred early in the program. Every morning a list of names would be called out—and a few disappointed (and perhaps secretly relieved) soldiers would fall out and pack their kits.

"Yesterday was the worst day," Yoni wrote to his parents later that month. "We exercised nonstop all day, and by evening everyone was thoroughly exhausted and praying for a good long sleep (i.e., four or five hours). We thought we'd earned it after being pushed so hard physically.

". . . But the officers had other ideas, for immediately after supper they started a night exercise which went on for a few hours. After the exercise, our hopes for a good sleep went by the board when a five-mile high-speed march was announced! . . . This is the worst thing in the army, worse than any running, because no rhythm is kept. You [have to] start running wildly to catch up with the others and close the gaps.

". . . Well, after the march, which was extended by an extra mile, we came back to the camp, and then again, instead of sleeping, we were put through a *titur*. (Titur means we have to run and fetch the cot, then the mattress, then the kitbag, then the mess tin, then put on our winter clothes, etc.—all in a matter of seconds.) That was really too much. We barely dragged ourselves along. We thought *now* they'll let us sleep; it was the middle of the night by then.

"But no, we were told we were having a 'Commander's Review,' which is a major inspection normally lasting three hours and requiring a full day's preparation. As a result, they kept us up till about 3:30 in the morning to straighten up our tents, tighten the ropes, clean up the grounds, and so on.

"After that, when we had only a little over an hour left for sleep, it turned out that it was our squad's turn for all-night guard duty. So we stayed awake all night through that *marvelous* night!"

In addition to the night maneuvers, the running, and the marching, there were arms drills, in which Yoni learned how to pull apart, assemble, and load a weapon within seconds, both in daylight and in darkness. There were also constant physical fitness workouts, shooting practice, obstacle courses, and—of course—mess hall and guard duty. The runs and marches were the toughest. They were performed while in full uniform and carrying backpacks filled with canteens, ammunition, arms, and other equipment. Sometimes the maneuvers included carrying "casualties" on stretchers, sometimes for as much as twenty miles—in these "rehearsals," the lucky guys were the casualties on the stretchers!

By October, the number of soldiers in Yoni's squad had drastically diminished. Many fainted from weakness and exhaustion and were forced to drop out of the program. "Only the strongest and most efficient remain," Yoni wrote to his brothers. "Here you become hardened or you break down. There is no middle ground. . . . I feel that I am now at the top of my form. No march, no run, and no physical effort is really difficult for me now." Shortly after writing this, Yoni's fitness was tested in a series of field exercises that combined all the skills learned so far in basic training and were carried out off the base, in the "field."

". . . The location of these exercises," he wrote to his parents, "was about forty miles from the base, and needless to say, we covered this ground on foot with all our equipment on our backs. Everybody arrived in poor shape and everyone was limping badly. I came through quite well (compared with the others) . . . since some of our group had trouble marching, the others had to drag them along—literally *drag* them! There were only six or eight of us who were able to do it. I 'adopted' a very nice fellow who weighs about 200 pounds, and believe me, dragging a guy like that is no easy task!

"This time it was firing exercises. All we did, day and night, was shoot, shoot, shoot. We shot rifles, Uzis, machine guns, bazookas, anti-tank guns, mortars, etc., until our ears rang from all the noise."

The remaining weeks of basic training were spent almost entirely in the field. In November, Israel's rainy season began, and Yoni and the other soldiers performed some of the most demanding maneuvers in pouring rain.

"After marching all night," Yoni wrote to his parents, "we arrived in an area on the border of the Valley of Ayalon. We got there in the pouring rain and pitched tents in the wet, muddy ground. That same day, we began exercises at 12:30 p.m. and continued with them until 7 p.m. in the rain, the like of which I swear I never saw even in America."

Yoni and his men were often soaked to the skin. Since the men only brought minimum gear into the field, they had no dry clothes to change into and slept in wet, saturated clothes. When some soldiers woke up, they were unable to move their limbs and had to be transported to a nearby hospital.

"I was so cold, I couldn't hold a match in my fingers to light a candle," wrote Yoni.

Finally, on November 27, 1964, basic training was ended, and Yoni was on his way to jump school. Yoni compared jump school to the light at the end of a long, dark tunnel. Every paratrooper looked forward longingly to it. The three-week course was the easiest part of paratroop training and the most fun.

The first two weeks of the course included ground exercises—instructions on how to enter the plane, how to sit inside it, and what to do from the moment the paratrooper entered the plane until the moment his feet touched the ground. Each step required a separate, difficult drill, which one had to know perfectly.

The third week was devoted solely to actual jumps—seven altogether, including two without battle gear and weapons and two with, and three night jumps. After successfully performing the final jump, which was followed by a march in full gear, the soldier received the red beret and silver paratroop wings that meant he was now officially a paratrooper in Zahal.

In late December, on the night before his final jump, Yoni was on guard duty. He was glad for the chance to be alone and have time to collect his thoughts and write to his family. In his letter, Yoni described what it was like to jump from a plane for the first time.

"There are thirty-six of us in our plane," he wrote. "Eighteen men are to jump from the right-hand exit, eighteen from the left-hand. I am designated to jump first, left side, plane number one. The doors close behind us slowly and the plane begins to roll. Its thunder turns into a roar and its roar into a wail. As it picks up speed, we 'help' it take off by shouting 'On! On!' and then burst into song.

"Suddenly the doors open, and immediately afterwards we hear the command, 'Attention!' which brings us to our feet, tense and ready. Once again the order is given—'Attention!'—and I stand for a moment in the door[way], in the 'ready' position, looking around. Far, far below is the ground. Ahead, just in front of me, I can hear the whistling of the wind and feel it chilling my hands, which are already outside. My head is raised, and I look straight ahead. My right foot is back, ready to give the kick that will catapult me into space. No time for fear. Everything has to be done just right.

"'Jump!' I hurl myself out of the plane, the floor slips from under my feet and I am out in space. I take the blast of the slipstream as it pushes me left toward the tail, and I feel myself falling down, down. I count aloud, 'Twenty-one! Twenty-two! Twenty-three!' It's important to stay alert and keep a sense of time. During this first jump you don't feel yourself falling so much, you're conscious only of the wind all around you that's chaining you and preventing you from moving your limbs. Your head is bent, your arms are crossed, and your legs are curled up very, very tight. The chute opens.

"I look up and see the canopy spread out. No cords are twisted, nothing needs fixing. I release the right side of the reserve chute and look around me. Behind me, all about me, parachutes are scattered. You no longer feel yourself falling; you are floating slowly, slowly, between heaven and earth. Now the landscape is different—quiet, silent, filled with a kind of majesty. It is virtually impossible to describe those seventy seconds in the air! It's undoubtedly the most marvelous experience. You're master of the world and—even more so—of your own self!

"The ground below grows increasingly larger—already you are only about fifty yards above it. The day is clear and there is scarcely a breath of wind. [There is] A slight drift to the right which you must stop so the chute won't drag you once you've landed.

"Forty yards . . . thirty yards . . . now the ground is drawing closer with ever-increasing speed and you get into the 'Prepare to land' position. You must observe all the rules. Your legs and feet are pressed together tightly, glued to one another. If both don't strike the ground with equal force, there's a good chance you'll break a leg. Your legs are slightly bent. Your head is lowered. Your arms tighten on the steel helmet.

"Twenty yards . . . ten yards . . . and then it's over! Landing, rolling correctly, and you're on your feet, running around the chute to grab it.

"You glance upward and there, across the face of the heavens, are scattered the parachutes from the planes that followed us; for several hundred yards around you can see figures dropping, landing, and immediately springing to their feet. Is everything alright? All landed safely. One sprained his foot; he didn't do everything he should have. Trucks take us back to the base. Over and done.

"We've jumped!"

7

An Officer

After a nine-day leave in which Yoni caught up on some much-needed sleep, he returned to the army to begin "advanced training" for the officer training course. This involved exercises such as helicopter and tank assaults and practice landings from the sea. Six months later, in July of 1965, Yoni completed his training and was awarded the rank of Corporal.

Yoni was then evaluated for leadership qualifications. During an intense three-day period, he took a series of psychological tests that determine a person's capacity to make difficult decisions, solve problems, and control and organize others. On the basis of his test results, Yoni was accepted as a candidate for the six-month officer cadet course.

Yoni was proud to learn that he had scored a 9 on a

scale of 1 to 9, but he agonized for days about whether he should become an officer. This meant spending extra time in the army and thus delaying his enrollment in Harvard. After carefully weighing all his options, Yoni decided that Harvard could wait, and reported for duty at Kiryat Syrkin, near the town of Petach Tikvah.

After the rigors of the Paratroop basic training, Yoni found officer training school easy and downright luxurious—living in a room with lights and running water, wearing pajamas and sleeping in a real bed with sheets, for six or eight hours at a time!

In officer training school, cadets are taught such skills as commanding a platoon in the field, navigating in the desert, and house-to-house combat. But the most important skill they learn is the principle of "Follow me"—a principle that Yoni would come to exemplify all his life. "Follow me" basically means that an officer always leads his men in battle, no matter how great the danger. No Israeli officer *tells* his men to attack . . . he *leads* them in battle. Other armies may use "Charge!" or "Forward!" as a routine battle command; Israeli officers say "Follow me!"

Yoni especially liked being a lot closer to "the action" in officer training school. Instead of practice exercises like attacking a post held by another platoon, the trainees studied maps and aerial photographs of actual enemy territories and installations. Suddenly, being in Zahal was no longer a game in which Yoni and his fellow soldiers were playing "war."

As his role as an officer in Zahal defending his country became more "real," Yoni's love for Israel grew. Every few weeks, when Yoni would get leave, he traveled across the countryside—usually with Tutti (Tirza) Krasnoselsky, a young woman he had known from the Gymnasia Ivrit and had started to date just before he entered the army.

He and Tutti toured the Upper Galilee in northern Israel, climbing Mount Meron and swimming in the *Kinneret* (the Sea of Galilee). They visited the Cave of Alma—awed by the vibrant, colorful stalactites—and the Dishon ravine, which—to their immense surprise—was full of rabbits! They backpacked through southern Israel and the Judaean Desert, climbing to the top of Masada, hiking across *Nachal David* (the Brook of David) and the mountains of Ein Gedi, making their way to the town of Arad, famous for its hot springs.

With every inch of desert he explored, every town he visited, and every mountain he climbed, Yoni's love and admiration for Israel deepened. He wrote to his parents, "All of these hikes and trips made a profound impression on me. Until now, I must admit, I never *felt* the country, if you can put it like that. I think Bibi felt it much more than I, and also Father spoke more than once of 'our land.' Never before have I felt this so powerfully. I knew the country existed, that I was living in it, and that, if the need arose, I would fight for it. But really to feel the place—the soil, the mountains and valleys of Israel—this sensation I have now experienced for the first time.

"I have seen and felt the beauty of the Judaean Desert . . . and the life of our ancestors in the oases of the desert. . . . I saw places of beauty, which were created before and after the establishment of the State [of Israel]. All of this, together with the special sense of life I have acquired in the army, has now become enmeshed in my being, creating the full circle of a life that is whole."

On January 4, 1966, at the age of twenty Yoni completed the officer training course. He was proud and happy to learn that he had been selected to return to his former paratroop battalion as a platoon commander. In addition to this honor, Yoni was chosen to lead the final training course exercise. But the greatest honor was awarded him on Graduation Day, when Yoni was named the "Outstanding Company Cadet," chosen not only by the staff but also by his fellow students, in recognition of his exceptional leadership qualities.

Later, Yoni wrote to his parents, "[I] heard the call: 'Outstanding Company Cadet—Yonatan Netanyahu.' I had to come to attention, call out 'Sir!' and then present myself in front of the Chief of Staff [Yitzhak Rabin]. [He] approached me, pinned the insignia on the lapel of my jacket, exchanged a few words with me, congratulated me on my achievements, then shook my hand and wished me success."

The moment was photographed, and Yoni soon had a prized possession—a photo of himself saluting Rabin. (Years later Rabin autographed the picture and Yoni presented it to his parents.)

In February of 1966, young officer Yonatan Netanyahu traveled to the Kelet to select the recruits he would command for the next twelve months, transforming

forty teenagers into hard-working, dedicated Israeli soldiers. His young charges were immediately impressed
by their commander, who not only kept up with them
in their strenuous basic training exercises, but outran
and outmarched them most of the time.

One of the recruits under Yoni's command wrote
later about his first few weeks in basic training. "My
first thought was: How did I fall into the hands of such
a tough commander? . . . I think our greatest fear of
Yoni was when he ordered us to run. . . . He used to
push himself to the very limit. Men used to drop out—
but never Yoni. If he made us jump into the water, he
jumped into the water. If he sent us on a run, he ran
with us. And when we had to run [carrying] stretchers,
he ran with stretchers."

A few recruits didn't take their army service seriously and tried to get out of doing certain chores and
exercises. Yoni knew how to deal with these offend-
ers—he had learned that the best discipline often was
no discipline at all! Once, when one of the men "col-
lapsed" during an exercise run, Yoni ordered the others
in the platoon to take turns carrying the "injured"
soldier on a stretcher back to the base, several miles
away.

When they got back to the base, the soldier jumped
off the stretcher, smiled, stretched his arms and legs,
and thanked his fellow recruits for the ride. The other
men were furious and waited to see how Yoni would
punish this deadbeat. Yoni's reaction was to let the
men handle the situation themselves—he figured if the
punishment came from those who had suffered, it
would be more effective. He was right. When the pla-

toon finished dealing with their practical joker, he became a model soldier who never gave Yoni or anyone
else any more trouble.

Yoni often helped the men with their personal problems, taking care to treat them as equals and as friends.
Most of his soldiers felt deep respect and affection for
him, and they were proud to call him *Ha Mefaked*—the
Commander. They knew that Yoni pushed them extra-
hard for a reason—he wanted them to be the best
soldiers they could be. They had reason to be especially
grateful for the intense discipline when—in November,
1966—an unexpected turn of events placed them in
their first real battle.

Yoni and his men, who were training outside of
Jerusalem, were suddenly called back to their base. The
base was "sealed," which meant that no soldier could
use the phone, send letters, or go on leave. Everyone
knew that something important was about to happen.

The platoon commanders were ordered to select a
few of their men for a top-secret operation. Yoni picked
fourteen of his men for the mission. That night, under
cover of darkness, a convoy of trucks left the base,
carrying equipment, ammunition, weapons, and soldiers—including Yoni and his select group of men—and
headed for a depot at Baathshela, only a few miles from
the Jordanian border.

As most Israelis knew, Arab *Fatah* terrorists—part of
the PLO (Palestinian Liberation Organization) under
the leadership of Yasir Arafat—had moved into the
Jordanian West Bank and had been carrying out a series
of terrorist raids against Israel for months. They had
blown up two buildings in Jerusalem and, only a week

earlier, had taken responsibility for the mine that had exploded in Arad, killing three Israeli paratroopers.

At Baathshela, the convoy drove into huge hangars where armored trucks were waiting. When the men were issued brand-new weapons, it didn't take them long to figure out that their mission was in some way connected to these acts of terrorism. Soon the secret was out. Yoni and the others were going into Jordan!

At the crack of dawn, Yoni and his men boarded one of the armored trucks. Seated directly behind the driver, next to his wireless radio operator, Yoni could give and receive orders at a moment's notice. All his men were fully armed with Uzis, grenades, and flare pistols. A few soldiers manned the heavy machine guns mounted on the truck. They were about to take part in the largest Israeli military operation since 1956, when Israel captured Sinai from the Egyptians. Their job was to advance to the village of Samua in Jordan, about four miles across the Israeli border, leading a ground strike whose mission was to blow up the houses in the village occupied by Fatah terrorists.

When they reached the edge of the village, they were met by enemy fire. Within seconds, the Israeli soldiers began shooting back. When it was their turn, Yoni and his men jumped off the truck, covering each other skillfully, just as they had practiced a hundred times in basic training exercises. Hopping fences and scrambling uphill, they quickly reached the village. It was then that Yoni learned that the terrorists had escaped. Slowly, the firing died down. Yoni took a brief count of his men—they were all there and OK.

The orders came for Yoni and his men to pull back

after checking that the buildings the terrorists had been hiding in were empty—another unit of the convoy had been instructed to destroy the houses. As Yoni's men went from house to house, it suddenly dawned on them that they were in enemy territory! It was one thing to *train* for raids into enemy territory, but to actually participate in a raid on enemy soil was something entirely different—exciting but frightening, too.

Their part of the mission accomplished, Yoni and his men headed back toward the convoy. When they were a few hundred yards away from the village, they heard a roaring explosion. Turning around, they saw that forty or so of the terrorists' houses had been blown sky high!

As the convoy crossed over the border into Israel and drove through the city of Beersheva, the commandos were met by cheering crowds waving and throwing flowers to them—the raid had been followed on Israel radio as it was happening, and the Israeli people considered the returning soldiers war heroes!

Two months after the raid on Samua, Yoni's platoon completed the basic training program. *Ha Mefaked* was torn by two emotions. On the one hand, he was happy it was over—the long, grueling months of hard work—on the other hand, he was sad to say good-bye to the soldiers who had been his "family" for the past year. On their last night together, Yoni and his men partied until dawn, singing and drinking toasts and taking a moonlit dip in the freezing Mediterranean. Before it was over, they made a pact to meet every New

Year's Eve at Dizengorff Square in Tel Aviv—a pact most of them would keep for years.

Yoni had enjoyed being an officer, and he had sometimes dreamed about rising up through Zahal's ranks to become a crack commander of an elite paratroop battalion. However, after much thought, he decided that he should stick to his original goal and, after thirty months of army service, he was eager to pursue his studies and earn a college degree. During the last weeks before his discharge on January 31, 1967, Yoni had taken entrance exams for several universities, including Harvard.

His parents invited him to stay with them in the U.S. until September, when his classes would begin, but Yoni had other plans. "I've decided not to return to America right after my discharge," he wrote, "but to stay on here for a while. . . . To come to Israel, to serve in the army, and to leave immediately? That's not the way. Or to put it differently: I haven't yet satisfied my hunger for Israel."

On his discharge, Yoni moved into an apartment in Jerusalem. Israel was in an economic recession at the time, and jobs were hard to come by, but eventually Yoni found work moving furniture—hard physical labor, but "a piece of cake" after serving in the army, and it paid well. He also sold and carted topsoil to farmers, and in a short time he was making enough money to pay his rent and live comfortably.

To keep fit, almost every morning Yoni ran over the hills of Jerusalem, and during his free time he often went on long bike trips. Once he and his friend Koshe biked all the way to Eilat, the southernmost point of

Israel. Another time they cycled for three days in the desert, up and down the hilly roads near the Dead Sea, with their sleeping bags and food supplies strapped to their bikes, riding for miles against a fierce windstorm.

Yoni also spent a lot of time with Tutti, who was also living in Jerusalem. Over the past two years, they had fallen in love. On weekends they would explore the countryside, traveling to a different part of Israel each time. In Jerusalem they shared an active social life, dining alone together or with friends and going to movies and coffeehouses at night.

When he wasn't traveling, exercising, socializing, or spending time with Tutti, Yoni enjoyed spending time alone reading. He devoured all kinds of books, including the classics. Three of his favorites were *Crime and Punishment* by Dostoievsky and Elie Wiesel's *Night* and *The City of Fortune*. At this time he also began reading his father's works, all about Jewish history, especially the Jews of Spain.

In April, Yoni received the good news that he'd been accepted at Harvard. At the end of August he would pack up and leave for the U.S. to begin life as a student.

8

The 1967 Six Day War

At the same time that Yoni was enjoying the pleasures of civilian life, the atmosphere in Israel was growing increasingly uneasy and intense as the Arab nations surrounding Israel—Syria, Egypt, Jordan, Iraq, and Lebanon—publicly defied the United Nations partition plan of 1947, which had made possible the statehood of Israel, and broadcast threats to destroy the little country and "[throw] all the Jews into the sea."

There was an outburst of terrorist attacks all over Israel. Syrians in the Golan Heights shelled the *kibbutzim*—farm communities where the settlers shared the work and land—in Israel's Hulah Valley. In Gaza, thousands of young Palestinian Arabs demonstrated in the streets, shouting "Death to the Jews!"

Then, in May, Egypt blockaded the Straits of Tiran,

an international waterway. Without access to the Straits, Israel's vital southern seaway was cut off from the rest of the world. Israel asked for help from the United Nations, but this time it was denied. The U.S. and a few European countries protested, but no one offered to step in and aid Israel. Meanwhile, as the Soviet Union continued to supply the Arabs with thousands of tanks, guns, and other weapons, it became clear that Israel would have to fend for itself.

The Arab countries of Egypt, Jordan, Syria, and Iraq had voted to join together and attack Israel as one enormous army. When Egypt moved their 100,000 men into the Sinai Desert in preparation for an attack, Israel had no choice—on May 19, 1967, it mobilized Zahal.

Because of the constant threat to Israel's security, every able-bodied citizen not only is required to enlist in Zahal at the age of eighteen but also must serve in *mieluim*—the Reserves—until the age of fifty. Even though he had just completed his army service, Yoni was recalled immediately because of the gravity of the crisis.

All over Israel, men from all walks of life—kibbutzniks, shop owners, teachers, engineers—were called up to serve in mieluim. With the men gone from the towns and villages, the women and children took over their jobs—everything from delivering the mail to cleaning the streets. Life went on, but it became impossible to think or talk about anything but the impending war.

Yoni was assigned to the 65th Paratroop Battalion. In

a camp located in a citrus orchard in the town of Palmachim, he and the other paratroopers in his unit waited. They had no idea where they would be sent—perhaps to the north to fight off the Lebanese, to the south to defend the Sinai from the Egyptians, or to the east to protect the border from Syrians and Jordanians. They did not know that the huge Arab forces planned to attack tiny Israel from all sides.

Instead of being put in command of a platoon, Yoni had been assigned as a "spare officer." At first he resented the older, more experienced men in his unit. They all knew each other, and Yoni felt like an outsider. Then, as he got to know them better—listening to their stories of past heroic feats in the paratroops that showed courage and dedication to Israel—Yoni came to admire and respect them. "I found here the best guys in the world," he wrote to his parents. "Fighters, each one of them! Friends and companions, each one! What a joy, meeting comrades in arms. . . ."

In turn, Yoni's fellow paratroopers were impressed by the twenty-one-year-old officer whom they called "the new boy" and by all he had accomplished at such a young age. At the end of May, Yoni wrote to his parents, "With the threat of war hovering over our heads, we're all united, concerned for each other's welfare, helping and loving each other."

"The morale in the army is high," Yoni wrote in another letter. "You might even say sky high! There are many married men here, some of them fathers, and not one among them wants war, but we all know for certain—we shall be victorious! If war breaks out, we will come out on top, both because we are better and because we *must* win."

Finally, on June 4, Yoni's unit received orders to move south toward Egypt. At the time that the orders came through, Yoni was on a twenty-four-hour leave visiting Tutti and her family in Rehavia. He made it back to the base only minutes before the unit was leaving. If his fellow soldiers hadn't packed his gear and loaded it onto the bus, Yoni might have missed the mission altogether!

Just before dawn, Yoni and the other soldiers reached their destination on the Israel-Egypt border. Quickly, they unloaded their gear, climbed into the foxholes they'd dug in the sand dunes, and waited for orders. Overhead they saw waves of Israeli aircraft flying into Egypt. In the distance they could see Israeli tanks creeping west over the border. The war had officially begun!

Yoni lay huddled for twelve hours in his foxhole that day, growing more impatient with each passing minute. He managed to scrounge up a pen and some paper and scribbled a short note to Tutti. "I'm lying dug into the ground, and a couple of feet above me the camouflage net is swaying. It's cool here in the earth, especially with the net hiding the sun. If there was no war going on here, and if I didn't have to go out and kill, and if I wasn't alone, without you, it would be nice here."

Hours passed. Finally, in the late afternoon the orders came through to move on. Yoni's battalion was to lead a breakthrough attack on Um Katef—the great fortified zone that defended the entrance to central Sinai—clearing the way for the Israeli tank battalions.

As the soldiers boarded the army helicopters to be airlifted to a site near Um Katef, word came over the army radio that the front lines were under enemy fire and bringing in helicopters was becoming increasingly dangerous. Only one more helicopter would be allowed to lift off. The soldiers in Yoni's unit would have to stay behind—except for Yoni! No one knew exactly how, but Yoni had managed to squeeze aboard the last helicopter, part of a 150-man troop advancing into Egyptian territory.

As night fell, Yoni and his fellow paratroopers trudged through the wet, sinking sand dunes of the desert. Their orders were to secure as much territory as possible on the way to Um Katef. Suddenly a convoy of enemy trucks rose up out of the darkness. As the trucks approached, the paratroopers blasted them with every bit of weaponry they had. Unfortunately the trucks were part of an ammunition convoy, and the barrage resulted in a chain of deadly explosions. Five Israeli soldiers were killed, and fifteen others were wounded.

They had accomplished their goal—the tank battalions could now finish the job—and the orders came to withdraw and return to the assigned meeting point. The paratroopers staggered back through the desert, carrying the wounded, their path lit by fires from the explosions. When they reached their destination, they lay awake in the dunes, waiting for relief, listening to the moans of the wounded and the roar of the Israeli tanks in the distance. Two of the wounded died that night.

When dawn came, Yoni and the other paratroopers learned that the tank attack had been successful—Um Katef had fallen. On the way back to Jerusalem, an exhausted Yoni scribbled a note to Tutti. "That's it. A battle has ended. I'm well and all in one piece. We left the expanses of sand strewn with the bodies of the dead, filled with fire and smoke, and now we are once again in our country.

"I am eaten up with worry for you," he added with typical concern. "Perhaps in a few days, when it's all over and we're together again, perhaps then we'll smile. Right now it's a bit hard. . . . Tonight, and maybe tomorrow or the day after tomorrow, we'll be shooting again, and again there'll be dead and wounded."

Two days later Yoni's battalion was mobilized into action again. This time they were sent up north into the Golan. During the nineteen years since the Syrians had taken this territory from Israel, they had been using its strategic location to shell Israeli homes and kibbutzim in the valley below. In the past few days, they had destroyed more than two hundred houses and farms. Women and children of the kibbutzim hid in underground shelters as their homes above burned to the ground.

Because he was a trained mortar officer, Yoni was put in command of a support platoon. Its mission was to cover three rifle platoons as they raided the Syrian village of Darbasheya, where the Israelis believed the Syrian shelling was coming from. When they reached the village they found it deserted—it had been flattened by Israeli bombers.

Waiting for further orders, Yoni's battalion and the others learned that another platoon had attempted to capture the Syrian village of Jelabina, about four miles south of Darbasheya. This unit had run into serious trouble and there were many casualties. Yoni's company received orders to move quickly to Jelabina, infiltrate the village, and tend to the wounded. Exhausted but determined, Yoni and his men set off on foot along the patrol road that ran parallel to the Syrian border. Scrambling through thorny bushes and over the rocky terrain, they crossed the border and reached the village outskirts. Finally, at dawn, they reached a crest overlooking the entire village. As they rested briefly, the orders came through to sweep the area, taking out anything in sight.

Then—no longer protected by the cover of darkness—as the paratroopers made their way toward the village, a group of Syrians suddenly charged at them, yelling "Slaughter the Jews!" and disappearing just as quickly as they had appeared. The paratroopers, taken by surprise, had been too startled to fire. Seconds later, two Syrian tanks roared out from behind a grove of trees. The Israelis managed to blow up one of the tanks and radioed for air support. Everyone ran for cover, hiding in the nearest trenches.

Moments later, a lone figure stumbled toward one of the trenches. It was Yoni, covered with blood. As several soldiers rushed to help him, Yoni whispered weakly, "You've got to do something—there's another man—Itmar—out there."

As the soldiers pulled off Yoni's equipment and shirt and staunched the flow of blood, which was coming from his left arm, he explained what had happened. When the Syrians opened fire, Itmar—the soldier next to Yoni—went down with a wound to the neck. As Yoni reached out to help Itmar, he was shot. The bullet had hit a nerve in his arm, causing terrible pain, but Yoni had managed to crawl across the scorched earth and avoid enemy fire.

After an hour's search for the missing Itmar, it turned out that he had only been grazed and had found his way to the dressing station on his own. Yoni was carried by stretcher down the hill to the company's command post and, from there, was transported to the nearest hospital, in the town of Safed. In the last hours before the cease-fire that ended the Six Day War, Yoni's arm was being operated on while the others in his platoon boarded buses and headed back to Jerusalem.

As all of Israel listened to the news about the war on the radio, they learned of the swift victories of Zahal in the battle to defend the borders of Israel. On the first day of the war—June 5, 1967—there was the surprise Israeli air strike that wiped out all of the Arab air forces. On the same day, word came that Zahal ground forces had burst through the Egyptian lines, advancing all the way to the Suez Canal. Finally, it was announced that Zahal had defeated the Jordanian Legion and captured territory extending all the way to the Jordan River.

Against all odds, and without any outside help, Israel had defended itself and won the war. Not only had Israel emerged victorious, it had also reclaimed the Golan Heights and sections of Jerusalem that had been in control of the Arabs since the cease-fire of the 1948 War of Independence.

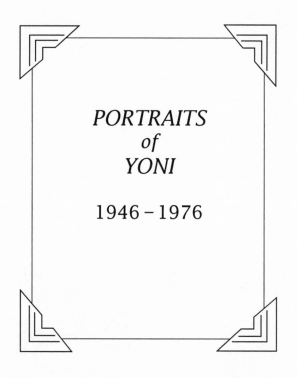

PORTRAITS
of
YONI

1946 – 1976

Yoni at age five, playing in Jerusalem's winter snow.

Yoni (at right) and two friends in kindergarten.

A Purim party in Jerusalem. Yoni (at right) is dressed as a clown.

An Israeli Scout outing. Yoni (age 16) is standing third from left.

*Yoni, at age sixteen, presenting the torch
of his high school's winning relay team to
Mordecai Ish–Shalom, Mayor of Jerusalem.*

*Yoni, surrounded by young campers at Camp
Young Judea (CYJ) in New Hampshire
in the summer of 1963.*

The Boys' Staff. Yoni is seated in front row, center.

"Go...man!" Yoni, at right, supervises a young camper on ropes.

One of the famous towers
engineered by Yoni.

Migdal dedication.
Yoni is standing between
two fellow Scouts.

Some campers and counselors at CYJ.
Yoni is in the top row, center.

*Yoni studying at Harvard
in the summer of 1973.*

*The last picture of Yoni, taken in 1976,
a few weeks before the Entebbe raid.*

9

A Student

Twenty-four hours after being wounded, Yoni was sitting up in his hospital bed writing a letter to his parents. Despite his constant pain, Yoni was in high spirits. "The war is over!" he wrote. "So much joy mingled with so much sadness overwhelms us all. How good that it's quiet now. It's no fun to run amid whizzing bullets and exploding shells, fighting again and again.

"Now I'm listening to soft music with Tutti beside me," he went on. "I have a bullet wound in my elbow, but don't be frightened . . . you mustn't worry about me. The main thing is that I came out of the war alive."

Like all Israelis, Yoni was elated at the outcome of the Six Day War. The mood of the country was euphoric and cheerful, but at the same time there was sadness about the casualties suffered in the war. Many families had suffered losses, but most Israelis agreed that it had been a "good" war for the country.

Several days later, Yoni was transferred to Haifa Hospital for a second operation. More than ten bone splinters were removed from his shattered left elbow, and his arm was set in a plaster cast. Yoni's major concern was that the injury would leave him disabled. However, Dr. Pauker, the operating surgeon, assured Yoni that his arm would eventually heal, although he warned that only time would tell whether he would regain full use of his arm.

After the operation, Yoni wrote to his parents that ". . . for me, it's enough to be alive. When you see death face-to-face; when you know there is every chance you too may die; when you are wounded and alone, in the midst of a scorched field, surrounded by smoke— mushrooms of smoke from exploding shells—with your arm shattered and burning with a terrible pain; when you're bleeding and want water more than anything else—then life becomes more precious and craved-for than ever. You want to embrace it and go on with it, to escape from all the blood and death, to live, live, even without hands and feet, breathing, thinking, feeling, seeing, and taking in sensation."

At the hospital, Yoni was visited by an endless stream of friends and relatives. He received so many gift baskets filled with fruit and candy that he joked he was going to open a gift shop or candy store. An unexpected and welcome visitor was Elliot Entis, Yoni's American friend. Elliot had come to Israel as part of an American

Jewish volunteer mission that was filling in for the men who had been called up to fight. As it turned out, he was working on a kibbutz close to the area where Yoni had been wounded.

Elliot remembers Yoni's impatience with the role of hospital patient as he slowly regained the use of his arm. One night, Yoni put on a white smock and disguised himself as a doctor so that he could "escape" for an excursion into town with Elliot. "The last thing Yoni wanted to do," Elliot recalled, "was lie in a hospital bed! He was always so full of energy. . . . We sneaked out the back staircase, went out for a decent dinner and then caught a movie." Yoni even managed to persuade Elliot to go bowling with him before returning to the hospital. Not an easy activity for someone without the use of both arms!

Perhaps the most welcome of all was Tutti, who visited daily, sitting by his side and comforting him when the pain caused by the damaged nerves became excruciating. During this time, their feelings for each other deepened, and they decided to marry. Happy and in love, they planned their lives together, deciding that they would get married on August 17, honeymoon in Paris for two weeks, and then leave for Cambridge, where Yoni would begin the semester at Harvard in September.

Yoni was discharged from Haifa Hospital on June 21. To earn some extra money before the wedding, he quickly found a job as a guide in a summer program for American students from Brandeis University visiting Israel. Naturally the young Americans were thrilled to have a battle-scarred Israeli war veteran, whose arm was still in a cast, as their guide!

Bibi, who was eighteen and preparing to begin his Zahal service in August, was on hand to help with the wedding plans. Yoni's youngest brother Iddo—who had persuaded Benzion and Cela to let him attend high school in Jerusalem—was also in Israel. Yoni was thrilled to have both his brothers with him at this important turning point in his life.

Finally the big day came. Tutti and Yoni were wed in a simple ceremony, with just family and close friends in attendance. Yoni's parents had flown in for the wedding, and Elliot Entis was still in the country. The ceremony took place in an amphitheater in the old Hebrew University on Mount Scopus in Jerusalem. It overlooked a magnificent desert landscape that revealed the vast beauty of the Jordan Valley and glimpses of the sparkling waters of the Dead Sea. Mount Scopus was one of the areas in Jerusalem recently liberated by the Israelis in the Six Day War, so the choice of this site for the wedding ceremony had a special significance for Yoni. After the wedding, Yoni and Tutti left for Paris.

From Paris, Yoni wrote to his family about the terrific time they were having, but Tutti later related that Yoni's arm was giving him a great deal of pain, and he was too ill and weak most of the time even to leave their hotel room. By the time he had recovered his strength, they were due to leave France for America.

Their first step in the U.S. was Elkins Park in Philadelphia, where they visited briefly with Benzion and Cela, saw a few American friends from Yoni's high school days, and picked up some pieces of furniture donated by Yoni's parents for their first home. Cela had found them a pleasant apartment in Peabody Towers, the married student quarters at Harvard, overlooking the Charles River.

At Harvard, Yoni registered for courses in math, physics, history, and philosophy. To support themselves, Yoni worked part-time at the University library and Tutti found a secretarial job at the Israeli Consulate in Boston. She also inquired at several local colleges, eager to continue her studies in psychology.

After the turmoil of war in Israel, life as a college student was very relaxing. Most of Yoni's time was devoted to his studies, but he and Tutti found time to travel and enjoy themselves, often going on weekend trips. To her husband's delight, Tutti proved to be a fantastic cook who enjoyed experimenting with different gourmet dishes every night.

Yoni's friend Elliot was also studying at Harvard, and they were happy to have such a good friend close by. And Elliot's older brother Alan was living in Peabody Towers. Like Yoni, Alan liked to keep in shape, and the two became running partners, jogging together every morning all over Cambridge.

That fall, Yoni wrote faithfully to Bibi, who was in the middle of his basic training in Israel. Yoni was thrilled and proud that Bibi had decided to join the paratroops, and his letters were filled with advice about everything from parachuting and navigation to healing combat boot blisters. In turn—feeling a growing homesickness for Israel and life in the army—he begged for details about everything Bibi "was up to" in the army.

"I'm filled with longing for the army when I read what you write about it," Yoni wrote in one letter. "I told you you'd be a good paratrooper and that the only thing that could prevent your becoming one would be—bad luck. So be careful, seriously. In every company there's at least one soldier who gets hurt by a stray bullet or a grenade that accidentally goes off, or some other foolishness. Make sure that it's not you."

Winter set in and Cambridge was cold and gray. Although his studies kept him busy, Yoni found himself becoming restless, as he followed the news reports about Israel. Terrorism was still rampant in the Middle East, and the tension between the Arabs and Israel was escalating.

He finally confided to Tutti that he didn't feel right about staying in America while his country was under the threat of war. After many hours of discussion, they decided that they would leave Cambridge when the school year was finished and return to Israel.

Yoni's college advisor at the time, Seamus Malin, remembers the day when Yoni came to his office and told him of his plans to return to Israel. "I shouldn't be here," Yoni had said. "This is a luxury. I should be at home. I should be defending my country. Harvard is a wonderful place to be, but I can't justify being here."

In the early spring, Yoni had a third operation on his injured arm, this time at the Walter Reed Hospital in Washington, D.C. In a letter written to Bibi several days later he confessed that he hoped to recover enough use of his arm to qualify for reserve duty in Zahal.

Yoni recovered slowly from the operation, which seemed to be successful, and he and Tutti began preparations for the move back to Israel. When the grades for the second semester came through, Yoni was pleased to learn that he ranked in the top ten percent of his class and had made the Dean's List.

On July 2, 1968, after a final vacation up north in Canada, Yoni and Tutti returned to Philadelphia, where they said a tender goodbye to Benzion and Cela and boarded a jet for Israel.

Yoni was relieved to be home again. In a letter to his father, he tried to express his deep love for Israel.

"I realize how much I missed that part of myself whose origin and place is in Israel. When I was in America, I knew my place was here, but not until I got here did I know how right I was. I belong to Israel, Father, the way Israel belongs to me and to you and to every other Jew. I belong to Israel now, at this moment, when a new explosion is hanging over us (although I hope it will not come to pass), at this moment when every civilian who has served in Zahal is being called up for two and three months of reserve duty, when the whole House of Israel is united in its determination to continue its independent life, and in its conviction that this life is ours by right and depends on our will and our readiness to sacrifice *everything* for its sake. That is why I have to be here—*now*."

Yoni and Tutti rented a basement apartment in the suburb of Kiryat Yovel in Jerusalem. Yoni got his old job back guiding American students through the city, and Tutti found work as a secretary. Her father had offered to put down a deposit on a piece of land in a new settlement in Jerusalem where they could build a house of their own—a project they figured would keep them busy for about three years. In the fall, Yoni enrolled in Hebrew University.

It seemed that Yoni had a lot going for him, but as time went on, he became more and more depressed. As he listened to almost daily reports about Arab terrorist attacks, he became convinced that Israel was experiencing a "calm before the storm," and that it was just a matter of time before the "war of attrition" was transformed into a real war—again.

As winter came and went, conditions worsened. "The atmosphere is tense, just as it was before the [Six Day] War," Yoni wrote to his parents in January of 1969. "I know for certain that we're moving toward a new war. It won't be a war that we'll begin, but one that the Arabs will. Perhaps the word 'know' may be too much, for I can bring no definite proof, but everything points in this direction. I know this just as I knew that the Six Day War was going to break out. Then, too, I was sure beyond a shadow of a doubt. . . ."

Yoni closed this letter with the news that he was planning to re-enlist in the army. His parents pleaded with him to change his mind, and Tutti begged him to reconsider. But Yoni had made up his mind—he could no longer just sit by and do nothing as his country was being plunged into war.

After a complete examination, Yoni was found fully capable and fit to serve in Zahal by the army medical board. Several days later he was called up for reserve duty and tested for renewal of his parachuting qualifications. He jumped twice with no problem.

On April 1, 1969, after signing up for two years of service, First Lieutenant Yonatan Netanyahu reported for active duty.

10

The War of Attrition

During the next few years, although war did not "officially" break out as Yoni had predicted, Israel was under the constant threat of war from its Arab neighbors. The world witnessed attack after attack against Israelis abroad. In airports throughout Europe, Asia, and the Middle East, Arab terrorists hijacked airplanes and took hostages, sometimes killing children and innocent tourists. In Israel, embassies and banks were common terrorist targets, and Jordan and Lebanon constantly carried out raids along Israel's borders.

To protect Israel, Zahal stationed specially trained units along its borders, mainly in the Jordan Valley and Golan Heights. Some of these units were reconnaissance groups called *sayeret* trained to go deep into Arab territory and wipe out the terrorists before they had the chance to attack. Their work was dangerous and top-secret.

Yoni was assigned the command of a newly formed Sayeret platoon. He went to the Kelet and spent a month interviewing recruits to train under his command, selecting men who had already completed paratroop and jump school training.

At first, like the men in Yoni's platoon five years earlier, the recruits didn't know what to make of their new commander. Yoni put them through the most difficult marches and the most strenuous field exercises, pushing them even harder than they were in basic training. At the beginning, with too much work and not enough sleep, there was a lot of complaining. However, the men grew to appreciate Yoni's strict standards as they were gradually transformed into outstanding soldiers.

One night, while on a mission on the Egyptian side of the Suez Canal, Yoni's men had a chance to appreciate his dedication and courage. An attack by Egyptian snipers, firing from all sides, had taken the Israelis by complete surprise. One man, wounded, lay out in the open, while the others ran for cover, confused and unsure what to do next. Cool-headed Yoni snapped out orders, restoring calm, and then—single-handedly—crawled through the crossfire to rescue the wounded soldier.

While Yoni's renewed military career was off to a terrific start, his marriage was suffering. Most nights, he did not leave for home until well after midnight, returning to the base at dawn. Yoni and Tutti barely saw each other anymore, and although they still loved each other deeply, they found themselves drifting apart.

Yoni felt as if he were being pulled in two different directions. He loved Tutti and wanted their marriage to work. On the other hand, to realize his dream of becoming the commander of an elite paratroop battalion, Yoni knew that he would have to make Zahal his top priority. All he could do was hope and pray that Tutti would understand and that their problems would eventually be smoothed out.

In the fall of 1970, at the age of twenty-four, Yoni became a company commander in *Sayeret Haruv*—the reconnaissance unit of Central Command in the Jordan Valley. Sayeret Haruv's primary function was to defend the Jordan Valley from terrorist infiltration. Yoni was proud to be part of such an important unit of Zahal, although he was sad to leave the men with whom he'd spent almost two years.

After selecting the ninety-six men at the Kelet that would make up his company, Yoni spent the winter training them for anti-terrorist operations. He joined in every training exercise—from marching five miles to crawling a mile or more with full equipment strapped to his back. It was always said of Yoni that he never asked his men to do anything that he couldn't and wouldn't do himself.

In January of the following year, Yoni and his men were selected for an important mission. Following up on a tip from local informants, Sayeret Haruv headquarters directed Yoni to intercept a Fatah terrorist meeting to be held on the weekend in a certain house in a mountain village near Hebron—the exact date was not known. For almost two months, Yoni and twelve of his men spent weekend nights until dawn crouching in the bitter cold on a hill overlooking the village, motionless and silent, waiting for a signal that the meeting had begun.

Finally, on a frigid Saturday night, the signal came. Quickly, Yoni and his team ran toward the village. When they were about forty yards from the house where the terrorists were meeting, an Arab guarding the place saw them and began shooting wildly. The Israeli soldiers, some of them in action for the first time, ran for cover—all except one. The other soldiers watched in awe as Yoni ran toward the house, leaping over a stone wall, and shot the guard. At the same moment two men ran out of the house. Yoni shot one of them but the other disappeared into the darkness.

Later, Yoni and his men were commended for the success of the mission. Except for "the one that got away," all the terrorists were captured. Yoni, who demanded perfection from himself, brooded over the fact that one terrorist had escaped.

For the rest of the year, Yoni was increasingly involved in training programs and operational planning, and he was away from home for weeks at a time. Living apart for such long periods of time was too much for Tutti. In March, 1972, after many discussions and heartaches,

Yoni and Tutti decided to separate; later that year they agreed to a divorce.

Yoni, devastated by the break-up of his marriage, dealt with his pain by plunging even deeper into army life. He was glad that his work kept him in the field for long periods of time. He was involved in anti-terrorist operations, which included all-night patrolling of the borders and long waits on stakeouts all over the country.

For Israelis, 1972 seemed to be the year of the international terrorist. There were hijackings, bombings and shootings at the hands of Arab terrorists in cities all over the world. At the 1972 Summer Olympics in Munich, Germany, for instance, Arab terrorists captured and killed Israeli athletes in front of the world.

Another terrorist incident became famous worldwide; on May 12, 1972, a Belgian plane that had taken off from Brussels was forced to land at Israel's Lod Airport. The plane had been seized at gunpoint by the Black September, an Arab terrorist organization; the terrorists had wired explosives all around the plane, forcing it to sit on a runway for hours at Lod. They threatened to blow up the plane and its passengers if the Israelis didn't release 317 Arab prisoners held in Israeli jails.

Yoni heard about the hijacking too late, and by the time he arrived at the airport to volunteer, a secret Zahal unit had already been assembled for the rescue attempt. Yoni pleaded with the commander—whom he knew personally—to be included but was told that the men for the mission had already been picked and that the rescue plans were set. A frustrated Yoni stood by and watched as Israeli soldiers, disguised as mechanics, fooled the terrorists into letting them board the plane. A stunned nation and hordes of reporters from all over the world witnessed the Israeli soldiers ambush the plane, kill the hijackers, and rescue the passengers. It was a special moment for Israel, and the reporters captured the rescue on film. The pictures were wired to newspapers all over the world, and Zahal was praised for its bravery and successful operation. To his great pride and delight, Yoni soon discovered that one of the "mechanics" was his very own brother, Bibi.

In June of that same year, Yoni found himself in command of an unusual and dangerous mission that made his personal problems suddenly seem very unimportant.

Israel had offered to release one hundred Arab prisoners in exchange for three Israeli pilots being held by the Syrian government. Israel was willing to make such an "unequal" exchange because they suspected that the pilots were being tortured. The Syrian government refused the deal because none of the Arab prisoners were as "important" as the three Israeli pilots. Frustrated, Israeli intelligence came up with a logical solution: they would capture a few Arab officials important enough to force the Syrians to make the swap!

The perfect opportunity came when a group of Syrian officers were scheduled to make a tour of the Lebanon border. A kidnapping was planned, and Yoni was put in command of a small force selected to carry out the operation. Sayeret units positioned on both sides of the Lebanon-Israel border waited and watched as the tour began, waiting for word to move. For two days in a row, the mission was called off because of the danger of being spotted by the Lebanese army. On the third and last day of the tour, the Israelis knew it was their last and only chance.

Yoni and his men were stationed on the Israel side of the border. As a convoy of Lebanese cars carrying the Syrian officials approached, they climbed into two Land Rovers camouflaged as Lebanese vehicles and drove through the border fence onto the patrol road on the Lebanese side. Dressed like Lebanese civilians they got out and pretended to be having mechanical problems with one of the Land Rovers.

Apparently some Lebanese villagers watching them suspected something was fishy and alerted the convoy, which started to turn back. Quickly, Yoni and his men cut them off. Opening the doors of the luxurious Cadillac in which the Syrians were seated, they knew they had hit pay dirt—inside were two colonels from Syrian intelligence, a brigadier, and two lieutenant-colonels!

Speeding back over the border into Israel, Yoni breathed a sigh of relief. The mission had been a success. Several months later the Syrian government finally agreed to the prisoner exchange, and the three Israeli pilots came home.

By then, Yoni was twenty-six years old and was now second-in-command of his battalion. In November of 1972, he rented a house in Tel Hashomer, near Tel Aviv, sharing it with two friends. However, he was seldom there, all his time being increasingly taken up by administrative duties that often kept him at the base until after midnight.

In the spring of 1973, Yoni took part in an important

top-secret mission in Beirut, a seaport and popular resort in Lebanon. *Mossad*—Israel's secret service—had learned that Abu Youssef—the leader of the terrorist Fatah organization—was hiding out in an apartment in Beirut. Yoni and a team of experienced commandos were recruited to capture Youssef and any other terrorist leaders they could find; they immediately began training and preparing for the mission.

A few weeks later, on the afternoon of April 10, 1973, Yoni and the others in his unit boarded missile boats in Haifa and headed north along the Mediterranean coast. That night, about a mile off the shores of Beirut, they let themselves down into several rubber rafts. They rowed silently, not speaking, the only sound the swish of the oars as they dipped into the water. After beaching the rafts on the sandy shore they walked quickly toward the section of the city where the night life was centered. Wearing sandals and shorts and colorful, casual shirts, they mingled easily with the crowd of tourists, passing restaurants and nightclubs and finally reaching the checkpoint where Mossad agents had several cars waiting.

On reaching Youssef's apartment building, the unit split up. As one Israeli dispatched a security guard and another stood watch at the building's entrance, Yoni and two of his men ran up the six flights of stairs to Youssef's apartment. Quickly they wired explosives to blow open the heavy metal door of the apartment, which was bolted shut. Suddenly they heard shots down below—they had been discovered! They knew they had to move even faster.

When the door blew apart, a surprised Abu Youssef

stood staring at the Israeli commandos and then turned and ran down the hall, locking himself in a room at the rear of the apartment. Because their orders had been to take Youssef alive if possible, the Israelis held their fire. After trying unsuccessfully to batter down the door, one of the commandos fired through the lock, and the door swung open.

When they entered the room, Yoni and his men found Youssef lying on the floor, mortally wounded by their gunfire. They left the dying man, grabbed all the files and documents they could carry, and ran for the stairs.

As they raced through the apartment entrance, they narrowly escaped the Lebanese police who arrived with sirens blaring in response to a neighbor's call. Yoni and the other commandos jumped into their waiting cars and fired in the direction of the police as they sped off.

Only thirty minutes from the time they had first landed on the beach, the Israeli commandos were rowing back to the missile boats waiting offshore. The mission was later hailed as a success, a feather in Zahal's cap, demonstrating that Israeli commandos were capable of carrying off a daring raid in enemy territory and in record time.

By 1973, Yoni had risen to the rank of major and had completed his stint as second-in-command. In June, 1973, after four straight years of army service, he was in desperate need of a change. Still determined to get his Bachelor of Arts degree from Harvard, Yoni applied and was accepted for Harvard's summer school program.

As soon as he received leave from Zahal, Yoni returned to America, renting an apartment in Cambridge. He was not far from Bibi, who was living in Boston with his new wife Mickey and was attending M.I.T. (Massachusetts Institute of Technology). After spending some time with Bibi and Mickey, Yoni took off for a three-week tour of South America before beginning his summer classes.

Back in Cambridge and busy with his studies, Yoni felt relaxed and happy for the first time in years. Miles away from the pressure of being in the army, Yoni enjoyed his simple life, one without night maneuvers, gun battles, and terrorist kidnappings. He especially enjoyed his courses in government and international relations, catching up on his reading, and spending weekends traveling with Bibi and Mickey.

At the close of September, a refreshed, rejuvenated Yoni flew home to return to his life as a soldier. "I am still in a glow from the months I spent at Harvard," Yoni wrote to his parents from Israel. "There's no question that the summer gave me a lot personally. It was a wonderful opportunity to widen horizons.

"Above all, shedding responsibility for a few months gave me a sense of freedom and lightness and allowed me to enter new domains: a new curiosity, a new interest, a different world, unfamiliar books, interesting conversations, staying in your company . . . all in one summer!

"Without a doubt," he added, "I'll return to complete my studies."

* * *

A short time later, on the morning of Yom Kippur, when most Israelis were in synagogue observing this holiest, most solemn of Jewish holidays, the Arab armies launched a devastating attack on the Golan Heights and the Suez Canal. It was an attack that caught everyone by surprise.

11

The Yom Kippur War

At 2 P.M, Saturday, October 6, 1973, Israel was officially declared in a state of war. As Egyptian assault boats headed toward Israel and hundreds of Syrian tanks crossed its border in the north, Israel faced the gravest threat to its survival in all its twenty-five years of existence.

Like thousands of other soldiers and reservists, Yoni was immediately recalled to duty. As soon as he returned to the base, he mobilized his unit and waited for orders. During that first day of the war, a day that seemed to go on forever, Yoni and his men listened to the radio, growing increasingly impatient to get into action with each report of yet another attack on Zahal in the Sinai and the Golan.

On Sunday, with still no word from Zahal headquarters, Yoni instructed his men to load up the convoy trucks with food and ammunition and head north. When they reached the Northern Command headquarters, Yoni and the others were stunned. Headquarters was in total disorder; caught off guard, the Zahal units stationed in the north had been thrown into battle totally unprepared and without any solid leadership.

Yoni learned that the Syrians had made their way south, all the way to Nafah—Zahal headquarters in the Golan. As Yoni and his men headed for Nafah they met up with Brigadier General Rafael Eytan, who was in command of the Golan defense forces. Eytan was more than happy to receive reinforcements and gave them permission to proceed.

When Yoni and his men reached Nafah, they gazed in total shock at the burned-out Syrian tanks, wrecked vehicles, and dead bodies strewn throughout the camp. Yoni told the commandos to prepare for another tank attack. The Syrians were no doubt close by and would most likely return.

Yoni was right. Two of his men were fired upon while scouting the area in their jeep. At dawn, Syrian helicopters were spotted landing in the same general area where the Israeli scouts had reported enemy fire. Yoni knew that his unit would have to strike quickly before the Syrians manning the helicopters could get oriented. His own special rules for carrying out a successful ambush were: Get in close, move quickly, and don't give the enemy a second to think. He was ready to put them to the test now.

Yoni and about thirty soldiers piled into their jeeps and sped toward the area where the helicopters had been sighted. As they were getting out of the vehicles, they were met by a barrage of gunfire. Quickly they took cover, rolling into the nearest ditch. Gradually the firing died down and it became almost unbearably quiet. No one moved.

Finally, Yoni stood up, then ran forward, motioning to the others to follow. Almost in unison, more than thirty men jumped to their feet and followed their commander. As Yoni led the assault, he fired steadily, pausing only to reload. The air rang with the crack of gun shots, shouts, and sometimes cries of anguish as the wounded fell.

The Syrian commandos had not expected to meet any resistance, and when the ambush was over, their death toll was more than forty. Yoni's unit had suffered only two casualties. An officer who had taken part in the attack later gave this account:

What I saw then was a picture I'll remember all my life—suddenly I saw Yoni stand up quite calmly, as if nothing had happened. With hand movements, he signaled the men to get up. They were all lying down behind cover, and he began to go forward as if it were a fire exercise. He walked upright, giving out orders left and right. I remember my thoughts then as his soldier: "Hell, if he can do it, so can I!" I got up and started to fight.

Yoni's second-in-command, Muki Betzer, who later became his deputy at Entebbe, had this to say:

The picture that stayed with me . . . is that of Yoni charging first with eight men behind him, storming twelve Syrian commandos and killing them all. This is a scene that I always see before my eyes—Yoni storming, firing and leading his men into battle, going before them and not giving orders from behind.

Yoni had won a small battle, but the news farther north wasn't so promising. Zahal units there continued to be routed, and the number of casualties and wounded was growing. The day after the ambush in Nafah, Eytan sent orders for Yoni and his unit to move deep beyond the Syrian lines to guard the Israeli tanks that were under the command of the crack tank officer Yossi Ben Hanan. Yoni and everyone in his unit grinned when they heard the familiar name. During the Six Day War, Ben Hanan had become famous—not only in Israel but also around the world—when a photograph of him appeared on the cover of *Life* magazine, standing waist-deep in the Suez Canal and waving a kaletchnikov he'd captured from an Egyptian soldier.

Yoni's unit moved into position, following about half a mile behind Ben Hanan's tanks. As the convoy crawled along the bumpy, dirt roads, the soldiers were tense—they knew that at any moment they could be blown up by a land mine or hit by a Syrian shell. Finally the orders came to halt, and the tanks roared into battle with the Syrian forces. By midnight, the enemy had been driven back more than ten miles into Syria.

The following morning, Yoni's convoy followed the tank unit even deeper into Syria in order to seize a vital position called El Farres, which was located at the Maatz crossroads between the Syrian cities Damascus and Kuneitra. As the tanks approached the crossroads, they were met by heavy enemy artillery fire. Within minutes, four tanks—including Ben Hanan's—had been hit! The entire attack could be heard over the army radio, and Yoni and his men listened with horror to the screams of Ben Hanan—"My leg! I've lost my leg!"

Yoni knew immediately what he must do. A rescue team composed of himself, Muki Betzer, twelve other soldiers, and a medic quickly boarded two armored trucks and made its way toward the smoke rising from the damaged Israeli tanks. Despite the continuing enemy fire, Yoni kept on going. He couldn't let a fellow officer die behind enemy lines. As soon as the rescue party reached Ben Hanan, the medic attended to his leg (which wasn't blown off, after all).

Minutes later, after a quick search for other survivors, the rescue team headed back to the waiting convoy. Within hours, Yossi Ben Hanan was recuperating in a Haifa hospital. Later he wrote this about the incident:

"We were hit and part of my force withdrew. My driver and I remained alone in the field. I was not in a very encouraging situation and had lost a lot of blood. The brigade commander radioed: 'Yossi, hold on! I'm sending Yoni!' He took a big risk coming deep into an area held by the Syrians . . . I owe my life to Yoni."

A year later, Yoni was awarded the Distinguished Conduct Medal by Israel's Chief of Staff, Motta Gur, for his brave rescue of Yossi Ben Hanan.

During the early hours of the Yom Kippur War, Zahal suffered a terrible blow when its observation post on Mount Hermon—strategically valuable because it overlooked all of the Golan Heights—was captured by Syrian commandos. Nine days after the outbreak of the war, when it became apparent that the safety of Israel was no longer threatened, the recapture of the observation post became a top priority of Zahal.

Yoni's orders were to position his unit high up on the mountain and provide back-up for the Golani infantry brigade that was to attack the post. Then, while the Golanis attacked from the front, Yoni's unit would cut off the Syrians' retreat from the rear. While Yoni's men were in training, they had navigated day and night over every ridge and valley of Mount Hermon, and Yoni—as a civilian and while on leave—had climbed Mount Hermon many times. It was difficult for him to take a back-up position in this operation, since he and his men knew the area so well, but being the excellent soldier he was, he could take orders as well as give them.

As Yoni and his men waited several miles up the mountainside, the battle between the Golanis and Syrian commandos erupted around them, continuing all that day and throughout the night. Early the next morning Yoni spotted three Syrians only a few yards away. As he gave the orders to shoot, the Arabs emerged from their "hiding place" and surrendered with their hands held high above their heads. Then, one by one, several more Syrian soldiers crept out of the woods and surrendered.

Later that day, Yoni heard the good news over the radio: The Golani Brigade had recaptured the Mount Hermon observation post. Looking up toward the peak of the mountain, he and his men watched as the Israeli flag was raised and unfurled. Then, a second report came over the radio—a cease-fire was announced. The war would end officially that night!

It was a bittersweet celebration. The Yom Kippur War was one of the bloodiest ever fought by Israel, and nearly every family had suffered a loss. During the two weeks that the war lasted, more than three thousand soldiers were killed, and thousands more were wounded. Yoni was grateful that he and his brothers had come through the war alive, but he mourned the many friends he had lost. Shortly after the fighting was over, he wrote about his feelings to his parents.

"This, no doubt, has been the hardest war we've known. At least, it was more intense, more frightening, more costly in dead and wounded, more marked with failures and successes than any of the wars and battles I have ever known. But it's precisely [because of this] that the victory achieved was so great. The army is strong and sound and has proved its ability beyond all doubt. And when I say 'the army,' I don't mean the regular forces, but the whole people. The regulars managed at heavy cost to hold the enemy. But it was the people who won the war."

12

A Battalion Commander

Before the Yom Kippur War, Yoni had never expressed much interest in Zahal's Armored Corps division. He had always been slightly uneasy with machinery and was more comfortable with what he felt he was best at—hand-to-hand, close-quarters combat. However, during the war, and especially during the rescue of Yossi Ben Hanan, he had been impressed by the tanks' power and efficiency.

Of the three thousand Zahal soldiers lost in the war, the greatest number of casualties occurred in the tank division. When Yoni learned about the severe shortage of Centurion officers, he volunteered to transfer to the Armored Corps and enrolled in the tank commander's course at the Sinai Armored Corps School.

Yoni soaked up every lesson on tank tactics like a sponge, determined to learn everything there was to know about tanks and tank command. He learned that Israeli tank commanders are normally fully exposed to enemy fire, standing in the turrets for the best possible view of the battlefield. He learned that to ride a turret means enduring pounding by the tank's heavy periscope, with plenty of bruises to show for it. He became familiar with all the different types of tanks—Israeli-, Russian- and American-made. And he learned how incredibly expensive it is to operate a tank in battle— forty-five dollars for every shell fired and five hundred dollars for every *hour* a tank was in use. Multiplied by the number of tanks in Zahal—at least two thousand— Yoni figured that tank warfare cost a small fortune.

In March, 1974, Yoni became company commander with a Centurion battalion. Shortly after that, when Syria began another "war of attrition" along Israel's borders, Yoni's company was sent to protect the Golan from Syrian commandos. Then, two months later, Yoni was placed in command of a Centurion battalion.

This battalion had suffered tremendous losses during the Yom Kippur War and was in desperate need of reorganization. Headquarters believed that Yoni could turn things around and bring order out of chaos. When Yoni arrived at camp, he was stunned by conditions there. The men were physically exhausted and lacked proper winter clothing and cooking facilities. They were living out in the open in the Golan Heights, on the outskirts of a Syrian village that had been captured by the Israelis in the Yom Kippur War. They were under constant fire by the Syrians.

Yoni's first order of business was to move the men to a new location, one where they weren't such an easy target. Next, he instituted a set of safety rules, including confinement to armored personnel carriers at night and mandatory wearing of protective flack jackets at all times. The battalion had been without leadership for some time before Yoni's arrival, and some of the men resented the tough new commander, complaining about the unaccustomed discipline and the seemingly endless drills and exercises. Yoni did not hesitate to transfer slackers out of the battalion and bring in "new blood." When questioned by some other officers about his actions, Yoni smiled. "Don't worry," he said. "I don't know how long it will take, but this is going to be the best battalion in the Seventh Brigade."

As the weeks went on, the complainers and doubters admitted that under Yoni's command the battalion was becoming stronger and morale was once again high. In a letter to Bibi, Yoni joked, "There are three battalions in this brigade, and mine was fourth place, slipping into fifth.

"Then, all of a sudden," he added more seriously, "people got down to it and started working at a normal pace (that is, *my* pace). I'm certain they are going to become an excellent battalion."

As his battalion gradually surpassed the others in the brigade and became its top unit, Yoni earned the respect of his officers and men as well as those over him at headquarters. His career in the military was flourishing, but his life away from the army had become almost nonexistent. Yoni lived for the army, and he barely took leave. "The army is my home," he once told a fellow officer.

* * *

Yoni remained close to his family, writing frequently to his parents, who had moved to Ithaca, New York, several years earlier, when his father had accepted a professorship in Judaic Studies at Cornell University. He also kept in touch with Bibi, who had returned to M.I.T. after the Yom Kippur War. When Yoni did manage to take a Saturday off, he enjoyed visiting Iddo and his new wife Daphna, who were living in Jerusalem.

Yoni wasn't unhappy about the narrow focus of his life; it was more that he felt something was missing. A healthy, young twenty-eight year old, he began to wonder if he were destined to spend the rest of his life "married" to Zahal. Then he met Bruria, an attractive nineteen-year-old recruit who had been transferred to Yoni's unit as his secretary. At first it seemed that everyone at the camp except Yoni noticed how bright and pretty she was. But as Yoni worked with Bruria and came to know her better, the two developed a warm relationship and gradually fell in love.

After Bruria finished her army service, she found a job as a flight attendant for the El Al Airlines and moved into an apartment in Ramat Hasharon near Tel Aviv. Yoni spent more and more time there. Often, they spoke of marriage, but Yoni wanted to take things at a slow pace. He still regretted the failure of his marriage to Tutti and didn't want to make the same mistakes all over again.

By the spring of 1975, Yoni's life—in the army and away from it—had improved. His relationship with Bruria continued to grow stronger, and he had received an unexpected promotion to lieutenant colonel. He could now say confidently and without bragging that his was the best battalion in the brigade . . . "the best in the Golan even."

That year, Yoni celebrated the first night of Passover at the base with his men, leading them in the traditional Seder. Because it celebrates freedom for the Jewish people, Passover was one of Yoni's favorite holidays. "The fact that the idea of freedom remained [through times of suffering and oppression]," he wrote to Bruria, "that the hope persisted, that the flame of liberty continued to burn through the observance of this ancient festival, is to me testimony of the eternity of the striving for freedom and the idea of freedom in Israel."

He described the joyful atmosphere of the celebration, with soldiers dancing and singing late into the night. "Last year," he reminisced, "I celebrated Seder with my men in a big tent near a *tel* [hill] in a Syrian enclave that was being shelled, and that too was a wonderful Seder its own way."

Yoni knew that if he remained with the Armored Corps, he could eventually expect a promotion to brigade commander, but he had never given up his dream to command an elite paratroop battalion. When the opportunity arose to realize his goal, he jumped at the chance. In his farewell address to his battalion, he praised the soldiers for their remarkable achievement. "You've all had a part in building up the battalion," Yoni told them. "You've made something out of nothing."

He then outlined his guidelines for building and maintaining a strong military structure. ". . . A number of things, in my opinion, are essential for the maintenance of any framework and I want to leave them with you," he began.

"I believe first of all in common sense, which should guide everything.

"I believe in the responsibility of commanders; a good commander—whether in charge of a tank, a platoon, a company, transport, or supply—is one who feels absolutely responsible for everything done under his command.

"I believe the buck should not be passed to someone else.

"I believe that there can be no compromise. Never compromise with results that are less than the best possible, and even then look for improvements.

"I believe, with absolute faith, in our ability to carry out any military task entrusted to us.

"I believe in Israel and in the general sense of responsibility that must accompany every man who fights for the future of his homeland."

In May, Yoni returned to the paratroops, this time as a battalion commander. He quickly fell back into a routine of long days and nights spent working at the base.

13

Secret Mission to Entebbe

About a year later, on June 27, 1976, Yoni was in his office at the base, seated at his desk among mountains of paperwork, when an urgent report came over the army radio: a plane carrying Israeli citizens had been hijacked! The soldiers in Yoni's battalion quickly gathered around the radio to listen to the chilling report. They learned that an Air France jet flying from Tel Aviv to Paris had been hijacked by Palestinian terrorists after a stop at Athens, Greece. There were 246 passengers on board, 105 of whom were Jewish—most of them Israelis—and a flight crew of twelve.

Later that day, the terrorists' demands were made public. In exchange for the hostages, Israel must release fifty-three Palestinian prisoners—forty supposedly being held in Israel, six in West Germany, five in Kenya, one in Switzerland, one in France, and two of the best-known non-Palestinian prisoners held by the Israelis: Hilarion Capucci, arrested for smuggling guns to Palestinian terrorists in 1974, and Kozo Okamoto, who murdered twenty-seven bystanders in a bloody raid at Lod Airport in May, 1972. The Israeli government was given until July 1 to agree to these terms or all the hostages would be killed.

That night, Yoni and Bruria discussed some of the alternatives Prime Minister Yitzhak Rabin might consider. In the past, the government usually had negotiated with terrorists, freeing Palestinian guerrillas and giving up land in exchange for peace that never came. Yoni said glumly that he was afraid the Israeli government would once again give in to the hijackers' demands.

In fact, however, behind closed doors Rabin and his Cabinet were considering the possibility of sending a secret rescue team to free the hostages. "If we accept the [hijackers'] conditions," Transportation Minister Gad Yaakobi told the other Cabinet members, "the Palestinians will escalate their terror and no Israeli leaving the country will be safe." Defense Minister Shimon Peres was also opposed to negotiating with the hijackers and called for military action "to counter [Israel's] image of a weak and indecisive nation."

Not all the Cabinet members were comfortable with the idea of military action. As they continued to debate about what to do, the July 1 deadline drew closer. Finally it was decided that Israel would have to agree to negotiate with the terrorists, because there was as yet no workable plan for rescuing the hostages. At the same time, Chief of Staff Motta Gur—along with Brigadier General Dan Shomron (the overall commander of the paratroops and infantry), Chief of Operations Major General Kuti Adam, and Israeli Air Force Commander Benny Peled—discussed with various representatives of the different Zahal units (including some of Yoni's men appointed by him to represent his unit) a master plan for rescuing the hostages. Finally a composite force was put together consisting of a reconnaissance unit, paratroops, Golani infantrymen, and an Air Force squadron.

On July 1—the same day that the non-Jewish hostages were released by the terrorists—Yoni was named commander of the reconnaissance unit responsible for storming the Old Terminal area of Entebbe Airport where the hostages were being held. His superiors— including Chief of Staff Gur and General Shomron— were familiar with Yoni's excellent military record and were confident that the clever young lieutenant colonel who had proved himself on the battlefield more than once, could handle the enormous responsibility involved.

Eager to take part in this mission, Yoni met with his staff at the base that evening to work out a strategy for the actual rescue. The Israeli engineering firm that had designed Entebbe Airport for Uganda back in 1972 provided sketches and layout diagrams of the area, but because the airport had since been rebuilt, these were outdated and inaccurate. Fortunately, Israeli intelligence was able to supply them with fairly recent aerial and satellite photos; and Major Muki Betzer—Yoni's close friend and the officer second-in-command of the reconnaissance unit—supplied many important details about the airport and the Ugandans that he knew from a previous assignment there. For instance, Muki knew that the Ugandan soldiers had great respect for Mercedes cars (Idi Amin usually rode in one)—this information led to Yoni's plan to use the Mercedes in a fake Ugandan convoy, in an effort to prevent the Ugandans from shooting in advance on the approaching Israelis.

The photos and other information supplied by Israeli Intelligence, combined with Muki's information, gave some idea of what to expect at Entebbe, but Yoni wished they knew more. Then, by a stroke of good fortune, on that same evening the non-Jewish passengers from Flight 023 were released by the terrorists and flown to Paris, France. During their three days of captivity, the released hostages had learned a lot about their captors and the layout of the Old Terminal. They provided detailed descriptions to the Israeli Intelligence agents who met them at Orly Airport—information that was immediately relayed to Yoni and his men.

Armed with this additional knowledge, Yoni and his staff worked long into the night, fine-tuning the rescue plans. The meeting broke up at 2:00 A.M., but Muki Betzer remembers how Yoni continued to work alone until after dawn: "At a certain point," Muki reported on Israeli Radio, "I suggested that we stop and go to sleep. Yoni agreed, and the smaller planning team went to sleep; but it turned out later that he remained alone in his office and continued to work on the plan. And, in fact, when he presented the plan at seven the following morning, I saw how far he'd carried the work from where we left off. There were many points of the plan we hadn't considered, which Yoni had thought through to the end. That morning he presented the plan—complete, perfect—down to the last detail."

Later that morning, although Yoni had had no sleep at all, he and his men ran through each step of the rescue operation at a makeshift replica of the Old Terminal. They practiced loading and unloading the aircraft that would be used in the rescue, mapped out every firing position and maneuver, and—after working out the seating arrangements in the Mercedes and Land Rovers—drove the vehicles toward the simulated target building, then tumbled out and charged toward the entrance, firing at terrorist "dummies" as they ran.

The same day, at his headquarters in Jerusalem, Prime Minister Rabin was becoming anxious, as Israel was running out of time. If a rescue mission was to be sent to Africa, it would have to happen soon. He instructed Gur to go ahead and finalize the plans.

On the evening of July 2, after Yoni and his men had gone over their part in the rescue several times throughout the day, a full-scale rehearsal was held with all the units involved in the mission. These included the Air Force squadron that would transport the rescue mission to Uganda, the paratroops that were to secure the New Terminal building—about a mile from the Old Terminal area—and the Golani infantry, which was in charge of guarding the evacuation planes. The paratroopers and Golani soldiers would also serve as backup forces, if needed.

When the rehearsal was over, Yoni conferred with the commanders of the other units and announced: "We must cut down the time it takes to get out of the plane and drive to the building." And although everyone was exhausted, they ran through the maneuvers yet another time, managing to complete them in under two minutes.

Later that night there was a final rehearsal, this time in front of Chief of Staff Gur and General Shomron. When the exercises ended, long after midnight, Gur left the base hurriedly, returning to Jerusalem to brief the Prime Minister and the Cabinet about the plan. Before leaving, he instructed Shomron to have the rescue forces ready to take off at a moment's notice when and if the Cabinet approved the mission.

After Yoni dismissed his men, telling them to get some sleep, he and Muki spent the rest of the night going over the rescue plans. Then, just before dawn, while darkness still covered all of Israel, a convoy of vehicles was mobilized and headed for Lod Airport. Altogether there were half a dozen Land Rovers, several Israeli-made armored personnel carriers (nicknamed "Rabbis"), and the Mercedes. At Lod, the vehicles and equipment were loaded on four Hercules aircraft. At noon the members of the rescue forces boarded the planes and took off for the Ophir Airfield at Sharm-el-Sheik in the Sinai Desert to await further orders.

A few hours later, although the government had not yet reached a decision to approve Operation Thunderbolt, Gur gave the go-ahead to take off from Sharm-el-Sheik and head toward Africa. If the government decided against the mission, the planes would be recalled home; if final approval was given, the mission would be able to proceed on time. At 3:30 P.M., the huge doors of the Hercules planes swung shut and the roar of the engines filled the air. Four minutes later, the four planes—along with a Boeing 707 jet carrying the airborne command center—were on the way to Uganda.

In the Cabinet Room at Tel Aviv, Rabin and the Cabinet reviewed the rescue plans presented by Gur once more. "Gentlemen," Rabin said, "Who is in favor of the decision which I shall now read?

"The Government resolves to approve implementation of a rescue operation of the hostages held in Entebbe, by the Israel Defense Forces, according to the operative plan submitted to the Government by the Defense Minister and the Chief of Staff."

Eighteen hands rose at once—the vote was unanimous. Chief of Staff Gur immediately jumped to his feet and left the room. Minutes later he had contacted the airborne command center aboard the Boeing 707 and relayed the Government's decision. Operation Thunderbolt was officially under way!

The planes followed the usual route of El Al (Israel's national airline) to South Africa—south over the Red Sea toward Ethiopia and Kenya. To avoid raising the suspicions of Ugandan flight control officers, as the convoy neared its destination two of the Hercules planes—those carrying Yoni and his men—flew ahead of the others and broadcast phony identifications. The first plane identified itself as an Air France plane delivering the Palestinian prisoners that the hijackers demanded, the second as an East African Airways flight scheduled to arrive in Entebbe in a few moments.

* * *

As Yoni's aircraft put down, ten paratroopers jumped from a side door of the plane while it was still in motion and quickly marked the runway so that the other planes could land. As the plane taxied down the runway, Yoni and Muki and several of his men were seated in the Mercedes—the remaining members of the assault force were crammed in the Land Rovers—watching the ramp of the Hercules slowly open. Then, as the plane came to a stop, less than a mile from the Old Terminal, the Mercedes, followed by the two jeeps, sped down the ramp. The rescue raid had begun.

When the convoy reached the tarmac leading to the Old Terminal, the vehicles were spotted by two Ugandan guards. One of the soldiers aimed his rifle at the Mercedes, cocked his gun, and ordered the convoy to stop. Thinking quickly, Yoni told the driver of the Mercedes to approach the guard slowly. Then, as soon as they were close enough, he gave the order to shoot, using silencers, and fired his own gun at the same time.

A split second later a loud shot was heard (its origin is still unknown); the men in the Land Rovers had no choice but to open fire, killing both guards. While this was happening, the Mercedes shot forward, stopping in front of the control tower, about fifteen yards from the Old Terminal building.

Yoni and his men scrambled out of the cars and started running toward the building. At this moment, the Ugandan soldiers began firing (there had been no shooting at all from the Ugandans since the encounter with the two guards). Perhaps because of this, the officer who was supposed to lead the assault force halted at the entrance of the building. Yoni shouted at him to keep on going, but the officer seemed to be frozen in his tracks.

Yoni quickly sprinted past the officer in order to continue the assault. Without a second to lose, the assault force commandos ran past Yoni and stormed the building, firing at the Ugandan soldiers guarding the various entrances. Yoni, in turn, ran toward an area outside the building opposite the main passenger lounge, where he could control the various teams.

Once inside, the commandos quickly shot and killed the terrorists and Ugandan guards surrounding the frightened hostages, who lay huddled on the floor, many of them still half-asleep. The raid had indeed been a surprise, and no one was more surprised than the hostages, who, after seven long days, had given up all hope of being rescued.

"Who are you?" they asked, bewildered.

"We are Israelis," was the welcome reply. "We've come to take you home."

Heavy gunfire continued to erupt outside the Terminal. Many of the terrified Ugandan soldiers—altogether about seventy were on duty at the time—fled, no doubt feeling it wasn't worth losing their lives for their Arab "brothers."

Many of the hostages, hearing the noise, were afraid of being shot as they left the building, but the commandos assured them that they would be well protected. The hostages were then escorted about 300 yards away to two evacuation planes, some in the Land Rovers and others on foot. As the hostages boarded the planes, Golani infantrymen formed a "human wall" on either side of them, shielding them from enemy gunfire.

* * *

While Muki was supervising the rescue inside the Old Terminal and preparing the hostages for the dash to the evacuation planes, he had received word that Yoni was wounded! Only moments earlier he had heard Yoni's voice over the walkie-talkie. What could have happened?

Later, he learned that Yoni had been shot in the chest as he was running toward his command post, at the same time that the commandos were storming the Old Terminal, only seconds before the terrorists were killed. While the rescue was still in progress, Yoni had been transported to one of the evacuation planes.

Fifty-three minutes after landing at Entebbe, the Hercules planes taxied down the runway and lifted off—destination Tel Aviv. It was only then that the freed hostages fully realized the immensity of what had taken place. Many sobbed with joy; others cried with relief—some sat silently, in a state of shock. The Golani infantrymen who were flying with the hostages laughed and congratulated each other, hugging and pounding each other on the back.

The joyful soldiers and hostages were unaware that, on the same plane, a team of surgeons and medics were trying frantically—and unsuccessfully—to save a wounded officer. Tragedy would mar the Israeli victory.

14

A Hero Returns

In a quiet area of one of the planes, Muki paced back and forth, waiting for word on his friend's condition. Finally, while the planes were refueling in Nairobi, an officer boarded Muki's plane and quietly told him the sad news: Yoni had died just before take-off from Entebbe. The medics had been unable to save him.

As word of Yoni's death spread, the soldiers stared hopelessly at one another. In the midst of joy and celebration they now heard the worst possible news. Muki buried his face in his hands, shaking with grief. Many soldiers sobbed openly. It didn't seem possible that Yoni could be dead. In their minds, he had been immortal. As the plane lifted off, there was total silence. Everyone's thoughts were on the brave young commander who had given his life for his people.

* * *

Eight hours later, after a brief stop-over at a military base in the Sinai, the convoy of planes landed at Tel Aviv's Ben Gurion Airport. News of the raid's success had spread throughout the country, and hundreds of Israeli citizens were waiting at the airport to greet the hostages and their rescuers. People danced and sang in celebration, waving Israeli flags and drinking toasts to Zahal. A triumphant rabbi blew the shofar and then led the cheering crowd in a chorus of *"Am Yisrael Chai"*—Long live the people of Israel!

The partying and rejoicing continued for days. Planes flew over Jerusalem, writing messages in the air like "All our respect to Zahal." In a speech welcoming the freed hostages and congratulating Zahal and its commandos for the rescue, Prime Minister Rabin said: "The basic principle is to fight the terrorists whenever you have a reasonable chance. You fight them in Zion Square in Jerusalem—or you fight them in Entebbe, but you *fight*. You don't give in."

In a country like Israel, surrounded on all sides by unfriendly if not openly hostile nations, happiness and joy are often mixed with sorrow. Four of the hostages had died—three caught in the crossfire at the Old Terminal and one an elderly woman who had been wounded and left behind in a Ugandan hospital, only to be executed by a furious Idi Amin.

And then there was Yoni.

Jews around the world mourned the loss of one of Israel's best, bravest, and most dedicated soldiers.

Yoni's parents, on learning of his death, had flown in from America with Bibi. They were comforted by dozens of relatives and Yoni's many friends, including Tutti and Bruria. It was amazing how many people had come in contact with and cared about Yoni during his brief life.

Two days after the triumphant return of the hostages, Yonatan Netanyahu was buried with full military honors at the Mount Herzl Military Cemetery in Jerusalem. At the funeral, Benzion sadly recited the *Kaddish*— the Hebrew prayer for the dead. Shimon Peres, Israel's Defense Minister, delivered a moving eulogy. Then, as the Guard of Honor fired three salvos, hundreds of soldiers who had come to pay their respect for their slain comrade wept openly, and *Ha Mefaked* was laid to rest.

Epilogue

In the short time that Israel has been in existence, almost every Israeli family has had its share of tragedy: a brother, son, or father killed in battle; a sister, daughter, or mother wounded in a bombing; an aunt, uncle, or cousin the victim of a terrorist attack. The Netanyahu family stands out because its tragedy is a symbol of national pride.

Yoni is a national hero in Israel, his very name synonymous with bravery and patriotism. Israeli children learn about Yoni in their history classes. Schools, public institutions, and streets have been named after him. Scholarship funds have been created in his name, and at Hebrew University in Givat Ram, a small garden at the main entrance flourishes in his honor. The Knesset—Israel's Parliament—voted to rename the Entebbe raid "Operation Yonatan" in honor of his memory. And

Yoni's former tank battalion base in the Golan has been renamed "Camp Yonatan."

Elliot Entis learned of his friend's death while reading an account of the Entebbe raid on the front page of *The Washington Post*. "Yoni was willing to put his life on the line," Elliot said in tribute to him. "That's quite unusual. My friend was a true hero in every sense of the word. I don't believe I'll ever meet another true hero, but I feel truly blessed to have had the opportunity to meet one in my lifetime."

Perhaps the words of Natan Sharansky—a Soviet dissident who spent nine years in a Russian jail just because he was Jewish—sums up for all Jews everywhere what Yoni's courage and dedication and sacrifice means to them:

"When I was in the Gulag, walking in the prison yard, I'd look up at a plane passing overhead and the guard would say, 'No point in looking up—it isn't coming for you.' But I'd always think of Entebbe and how, just once, the plane *had* been for me. 'Yoni' and 'Entebbe' were code words that meant 'One day you will be saved.'"

IMPORTANT DATES

1946   *March 13.* Birth of Yonatan Netanyahu in New York City.

1948   *May 14.* The State of Israel is established.
        November. Yoni's family moves to Israel.

1950   Yoni's brother Binyamin (Bibi) is born.

1952   Yoni's brother Iddo is born.

1957   Yoni's father receives a professorship in Philadelphia, Pennsylvania, and the family moves back to America.

1959   The Netanyahus return to Israel.

1963   The Netanyahus move to Elkins Park, Pennsylvania. Yoni enrolls in Cheltenham High School.

1964   *June.* Yoni graduates Cheltenham High with honors, then returns to Israel to begin service in Zahal.

1964   *August 10.* Yoni reports to Zahal recruitment camp.
        August. Yoni joins the Paratroopers.

Important Dates

1965   *July.* Yoni is promoted to Corporal.

1966   *January 5.* Yoni graduates Officer's School, and is named Outstanding Company Cadet.

1966   *February.* Yoni is put in command of a platoon battalion.

1967   *January 1.* Yoni is promoted to First Lieutenant.

1967   *January 31.* Yoni is discharged from Zahal and takes the entrance examination for Harvard University.

1967   *June 5.* The Six Day War begins. Yoni is wounded in the elbow during a battle in the Golan Heights.

1967   *August 17.* Yoni marries Tutti (Tirza) Krasnoselsky.

1967   *September 1.* Yoni and Tutti arrive in Cambridge, Massachusetts. Yoni begins first semester at Harvard.

1968   *July 8.* Yoni and Tutti return to Israel.

1969   *April 1.* Yoni re-enlists in Zahal and becomes a *sayeret* platoon commander.

1970   *March 1.* Yoni is promoted to the rank of Captain.

1972   *March.* Yoni and Tutti separate and are divorced later that year.

1972   *Spring.* Yoni participates in a famous raid on terrorist headquarters in Beirut, Lebanon.

1973   *May 5.* Yoni achieves the rank of Major.

1973   *June.* Yoni returns to America alone and attends Harvard University summer school.

1973   *October 6.* The Yom Kippur War begins. Yoni commands a unit that battles Syrian forces in Nafah in the Golan Heights. Near the end of the war, Yoni's unit defends Zahal behind Syrian lines and rescues tank officer Yossi Ben Hanan.

1974   Yoni receives the Distinguished Conduct Medal from Zahal for rescuing Yossi Ben Hanan.

1974   *March 1.* Yoni becomes a Centurion tank company commander, stationed in the Golan Heights.

1974   *April 27.* Yoni becomes a tank battalion commander.

1974   *November.* Yoni meets and falls in love with Bruria.

1975   *April 15.* Yoni is promoted to Lieutenant Colonel.

1975   *May 15.* Yoni returns to the Paratroops to command a battalion.

1976   *June 27.* Air France Flight 023 is hijacked from Athens, Greece, and taken to Entebbe, Uganda. One hundred and five Jewish passengers are held hostage at Entebbe Airport.

1976   *July 1.* Yoni takes part in Zahal's plans to raid Entebbe and rescue the hostages.

1976   *July 3.* Operation Thunderbolt, Zahal's secret rescue mission, leaves for Entebbe.

1976   *July 4.* Yoni is shot in the chest by a Ugandan soldier during the rescue raid. He dies en route to Israel.

1976   *July 6.* During the military funeral services for Yoni at Mount Herzl Cemetery, a eulogy is delivered by Israel's Defense Minister Shimon Peres.

GLOSSARY OF HEBREW TERMS

Arazim "The Cedars"—the name of Yoni's Israeli Scout troop.

Ha Mefaked "The Commander"—used as a term of respect and affection by Yoni's men.

Kelet Transit camp in Zahal.

kibbutzim Israeli farm communities, where settlers share the work and land.

Knesset Israel's Parliament.

Mieluim Zahal reserves.

Mossad Israel's secret service.

sayeret Zahal reconnaissance unit.

Titur A series of strenuous training exercises carried out by recruits in Zahal.

Zahal Short for *Zvah Hagannah L'Yisrael*—Israel Defense Army.

INDEX

Note: Page numbers in italics indicate photographs or maps.

Adam, Kuti, 98
Air France Flight 023
  flight plan of, 2–3
  hijacking of, 1, 3–7, 96
Amin, Idi, 6, 7, 99, 107
Arafat, Yasir, 43
Arazim, 20, 21

Ben Hanan, Yossi, 86, 87, 90
Betzer, Muki, 85–86, 98–100,
  101, 105, 106

Camp Yonatan, 110
Camp Young Judaea, 22–24
Capucci, Hilarion, 97

Darbasheya, Syria, 53–54
Dropsie College, 12, 18

Egypt, in Six Day War, 48, 49,
  51, 55

Entebbe Airport
  Air France Flight 023 lands at,
  4
  hostages at
    deaths among, 107
    Jewish, 6–7
    release of, 7, 99
    rescue of, 104–105
    treatment of, 4–5
  Old Terminal of, 4, 7, 8, 98,
    99, 100, 103, 104, 105
  raid on, 5, 96–105 (*see also*
    Operation Thunderbolt)
  renamed "Operation
    Yonatan," 109
Entis, Elliot, 22, 23–24, 65–66,
  67, 68, 110
Eytan, Rafael, 84, 86

Fatah terrorists, 43–45, 75

Golan Heights, 53, 56, 82
Gur, Motta, 98, 101, 102

117

Hijacking
    of Air France Flight 023, 1,
        3–4, 96
    of Belgian plane, 76–77
Hitler, Adolf, 12

Iraq, in Six Day War, 48, 49
Israel, State of
    establishment of, 14
    map of, 26
Israeli Defense Army. See Zahal
Israeli Scouts, 17

Jabotinsky, Vladimir, 12
Jelabina, Syria, 54
Jordan, in Six Day War, 48, 49, 55

Karpeles, Koshe, 21, 22, 46
Kelet, 27, 28
Kibbutzim, 48
Knesset, 109
Koubeisi, Basil el-, 3, 4
Krasnoselsky, Tutti (Tirza), 51,
        53, 64. See also Netanyahu,
        Tutti
    marries Yoni, 67
    plans to marry Yoni, 66
    travels with Yoni, 40, 47

Lod Airport, terrorism at, 76, 97

Malin, Seamus, 69
Mieluim, 49
Mileikowsky, Benzion (Yoni's
        father). See also Netanyahu,
        Benzion
    birth of, 11
    changes surname to
        Netanyahu, 12
    moves to Palestine, 11
Mileikowsky, Nathan (Yoni's
        grandfather), 10, 11
Mileikowsky, Sarah (Yoni's
        grandmother), 11
Mossad, 79

Mount Hermon, recapture of,
        87–88

Netanyahu, Benzion (Yoni's
        father). See also
        Mileikowsky, Benzion
    accepts professorship
        at Cornell University, 93
        at Dropsie College, 18
    arrives in America, 12
    attends Yoni's wedding, 67
    becomes editor
        of Encyclopaedia Judaica, 20
        of Hebrew Encyclopedia, 15
    buys house in Israel, 16
    education of, 12
    marries Cela Segal, 13
    moves to Israel, 14–15
    writes thesis, 14
    Yoni born to, 10, 13
    at Yoni's funeral, 108
    as Zionist, 12
Netanyahu, Binyamin (Bibi)
        (Yoni's brother)
    attends M.I.T., 81, 93
    attends Yoni's wedding, 67
    birth of, 15
    childhood of, 16
    in hijacking rescue of 1972, 77
    joins Paratroops, 68
Netanyahu, Cela (Yoni's
        mother). See also Segal, Cela
    attends Yoni's wedding, 67
    buys house in Israel, 16
    moves to Israel, 14–15
    Yoni born to, 10, 13
Netanyahu, Daphna (Yoni's
        sister-in-law), 93
Netanyahu, Iddo (Yoni's
        brother), 93
    attends Yoni's wedding, 67
    birth of, 15–16
Netanyahu, Mickey (Yoni's
        sister-in-law), 81

Netanyahu, Tutti (Yoni's wife).
    See also Krasnoselsky, Tutti
    (Tirza)
  divorces Yoni, 76
  marital problems of, 74
  returns to Israel, 70
  works for Israeli Consulate, 68
Netanyahu, Yonatan (Yoni)
  accepted at Harvard
    University, 47
  athletic ability of, 16, 24
  Bar Mitzvah of, 19
  birth of, 10, 13
  at Camp Young Judaea,
    22–24, *60–62*
  childhood of
    in America, 18–19
    in Israel, 15–17, *58, 59*
  death of, 106
  decides to leave Harvard
    University, 69
  divorces Tutti, 76
  education of
    at Harvard University, *63*,
      67–70, 80–81
    at Hebrew University, 71
    high school, 19–22, 24, *60*
  expresses love of Israel,
    40–41, 70
  funeral of, 108
  graduates from Cheltenham
    High School, 25
  homesick for Israel, 19, 21, 68
  as Israeli Scout, 17, 20, *59*
  and love of reading, 15, 47
  marital problems of, 73–74
  marries Tutti Krasnoselsky, 67
  meets Bruria, 93
  moves to Israel, 14–15
  as national hero, 109–110
  as natural leader, 16
  plans to marry Tutti
    Krasnoselsky, 66
  portraits of, *57–63*

  religious observances of,
    16–17, 23–24, *59*, 94
  returns to America
    in 1957, 18
    in 1963, 20
    in 1967, 67
    in 1973, 81
  returns to Israel
    in 1959, 19
    in 1964, 25
    in 1968, 70
  as tour guide for American
    students, 66, 70
  travels with Tutti (Tirza)
    Krasnoselsky, 40, 47
  undergoes third arm
    operation, 69
  in Zahal, *63*
    anti-terrorist operations,
      76–80
    basic training, 30–34
    becomes major, 80
    becomes Paratroops
      battalion commander, 95
    commands Sayeret platoon,
      73
    commands tank battalion,
      91–94
    declines Air Force service, 28
    Entebbe rescue, 7–9, 98–105
    joins Paratroops, 29
    named Outstanding
      Company Cadet, 41
    as platoon commander,
      41–45
    promoted to corporal, 38
    promoted to lieutenant
      colonel, 94
    raid on Samua, 44–45
    receives discharge, 46
    receives Distinguished
      Conduct Medal, 87
    receives officer training,
      39–41
    receives tests, 27–28

Index

recuperates from bullet wound, 64–66
re-enlists in 1969, 71
as Sayeret Haruv commander, 74–75
shot at Entebbe, 105
Six Day War, 48–56
starts jump school, 34–37
wounded in Six Day War, 54–55
Yom Kippur War, 83–89

Okamoto, Kozo, 97
Old Terminal of Entebbe Airport, 4, 7, 8, 98, 99, 100, 103, 104, 105, 5
Operation Thunderbolt, 7–8, 101, 102. See also Entebbe Airport, raid on
assault force of, 8, 103–104
blocking force of, 8
flight plan of, 2–3

Palestine, 11, 13
Palestinian Liberation Organization (PLO), 43
Paratroops, 29, 30
Peled, Benny, 98
Peres, Shimon, 97, 108
Popular Front for the Liberation of Palestine, 5

Rabin, Yitzhak, 41, 97, 100, 102, 107

Safed, 11
Sayeret, 72–73
Sayeret Haruv, 74
Segal, Benjamin (Yoni's grandfather), 13
Segal, Cela (Yoni's mother). See also Netanyahu, Cela
birth of, 13
marries Benzion Netanyahu, 13

Segal, Malkah (Yoni's grandmother), 13
Sharansky, Natan, 110
Shomron, Dan, 98, 101
Six Day War, 48–56, 64
Suez Canal, attacked by Arabs, 82
Syria
Israeli pilots held by, 77–78
in Six Day War, 48, 49, 53, 54
in Yom Kippur War, 83, 84, 85, 86, 88

Terrorism
on Air France Flight 023, 1, 3–4, 96 (see also Entebbe Airport)
on Belgian plane, 76–77
by Fatah, 43–45, 75
against Israel, 72, 76
Titur, 31–32

Uganda, 4, 6, 8, 98, 100, 102
Um Katef, in Six Day War, 51–52, 53

Yaakobi, Gad, 97
Yishuv, 11
Yom Kippur War, 82–89
Youssef, Abu, 79–80

Zahal
anti-terrorist protection by, 72–73
in hijacking rescue of 1972, 76, 77
mandatory service in, 25, 49
in Operation Thunderbolt, 8
in Six Day War, 55–56
in Yom Kippur War, 83–84, 86, 87, 88, 90
Zionism, 10–11, 12, 13
Zvah Hagannah L'Yisrael. See Zahal